Planned
ALL ALONG

by

Myca Belknap

Firebrands 616 Incorporated

Wyoming, Michigan

All Scripture referenced is from the King James Version unless otherwise noted. The Holy Bible, King James Version. Cambridge Edition: 1769

CSB, Christian Standard Bible®, Copyright © 2017 by Holman Bible Publishers. Used by permission. Christian Standard Bible•, and CSB® are federally registered trademarks of Holman Bible Publishers.

ESV, The English Standard Version Bible: Containing the Old and New Testaments with Apocrypha. (2009). Oxford University Press.

The Mirror Bible. By Francois Du Toit. © 2012 by Mir-rorword Publishing.

NASB, New American Standard Bible. La Habra, CA: Foundation Publications, for the Lockman Foundation, 1971. Print.

NIV, The Holy Bible, New International Version. Grand Rapids: Zondervan House, 1984. Print.

NKJV, New King James Version. Scripture taken from the New King James Version®. Copyright © 1982 by Thomas Nelson. Used by permission.

NLT, Holy Bible: New Living Translation. Wheaton, Ill: Tyndale House Publishers, 2004.

Additional Works Referenced

Strong's Concordance, Strong, James. Strong's Exhaustive Concordance of the Bible. Abingdon Press, 1890. Print.

All rights reserved.

© 2021 Myca & David Belknap, Firebrands 616 Incorporated

Firebrands 616 Ministries Publishing www.firebrands616.com

Cover design, layout & editing by David Belknap

© 2021 Decibolic LLC www.decibolic.com

Preface

The following came to me as I was awaking from a dream early one Saturday morning. In this dream I was with a group of fellow women in ministry and we were being addressed by another minister who I have known for most of my life.

The time has come, yes it's already here, that the Word of the Lord the shining of His bride is coming not from the gifts but from the everyday person. It's not that the gifts, the pastors and leaders won't shine. Oh they will shine, but they will shine as the bride, the person not the gift.

The Word of the Lord and the Glory of the Bride will again come from those who are ordinary: the fisher, the postal clerk, the store clerk, the housekeeper, and the student. The lawyer, the school teacher, the highway patrol officer, both the overlooked and unexpected will come into the light with direction and revelation that is revolutionary and out of sight. The fresh and the revolutionary is not in a pulpit or on a TV screen. Don't look to the known, the famous, and usual. It is found in the hearts, minds, souls, and hands of the ones on the streets.

Fishers of men, even tax collectors, ordinary folk, like Jesus' disciples of old are hearing "Come, follow Me!" Arise and turn the status quo on its ear. You carry the light and revelation of the Lord's year. Not a year as in a number of days, but a year as in a cycle of seasons that repeats (winter, spring, summer, fall). A year as in a growing process with times of rest, new life, growth, and letting go of what is no longer necessary to make room for new life after another season of rest. Not a year or cycle of fear, destruction, and woe. A "year" or cycle of love, light, and unity to grow. For you know the Shepherd and you know His voice.

He leads gently and not with threats. Calling patiently, with a whisper and still small voice. Your Shepherd enters in with the flock, and does not stand above, far away, looking on. Your Shepherd does not grandstand, self promote, or make flashy claims.

What of the miracles? What about signs, wonders and such? Remember an evil and adulterous generation seeks after signs. Signs will happen, they are a byproduct of eternal life. Natural cannot help but respond to Spiritual. Signs and Wonders will not be the hallmark, but lives changed, for ego must surrender to reflect the image and likeness of the eternal one. Like the loaves and the fish, miracles and signs will happen in and through the hands of the many, in the crowd, who are feeding the hungry followers of truthful words of life. No one disciple could take the credit, all they knew is that Jesus blessed it.

So shall be this new normal. All any individual will be able to claim is to be a part of something impossible that became possible because Jesus blessed it.

Table of Contents

Preface	*3*
Introduction	*6*
1. God Is Love	*10*
2. Life is Motion	*21*
3. Stranger in a Strange Land	*31*
4. First Things First	*36*
5. A New Home	*42*
6. Painting the Picture of Hope	*49*
7. Identity	*57*
8. Everyday Miracles	*64*
9. Against All Hope	*70*
10. Blessed to Be a Blessing	*76*
11. Identity Crisis	*83*
12. What is Your Backstory?	*89*
13. Faith, the Journey	*97*
14. From Obedience to Reality	*102*
15. Encounter	*107*
16. Call Me "Shem"	*114*
17. Planned All Along	*120*
Confession of Faith	*125*

Introduction

How is it that when some people face seemingly insurmountable obstacles and horrific situations they rise above while others fall into despair and flounder in endless struggle after struggle? The Bible contains numerous stories about the heroes of faith defeating Goliaths, parting Red Seas, and changing their station from Slave to Ruler. These were ordinary people whose struggle and triumph became the stuff of legends. Many were thrust into hopeless situations. Yet, somehow, rather than crumble under the pressure they rose and flourished. A revelation took root and brought forth something beautiful. Proverbial desert roses.

These examples were written for us. Their stories were meant to encourage and inspire us through our struggles and toward our own greatness. Each one reveals not only a journey but spiritual realities, if we have eyes to see them. Over time their stories may have been sensationalized into some kind of ethereal, magical, fantasy that raises them to superhuman status, but this was not always the case. Perhaps we sensationalize those who overcome out of our own fear of failure. It's easier to think that they are special (and we are not) so we are not special enough to try to bloom in our own desert places. We remain victims of often hopeless circumstances and cannot not imagine that God will flow through us in our brokenness.

This sensationalism coupled with our current climate of rampant deceit in both the religious and political arenas have made these ancient believers seem less ordinary and allowed us to convince ourselves that they are just stories and do not apply to real life. Though we may claim the inerrant truth of the Bible, in practice we have treated these Bible stories like fantasies, bedtime soothers, and entertainment pieces. In this era of intellectualism, realism, and modernism, we have lost the spiritual qualities and much of the wonder and mystery of our heroic predecessors. Some spiritual or religious leaders have taught that the secret to their successes involves much scripture quoting or confession, devil battling, holy living, fasting, sacrificial offerings, and an undisclosed amount of time spent in the "right kind" of prayer. This use of our spiritual senses to manipulate a seemingly unwilling God into doing our bidding could not be further from our Biblically based roots.

There is nothing wrong with quoting or confessing scripture. There is a place for God's sovereignty. There certainly is a "devil" to battle, and we wholeheartedly want to reflect the purity of our Creator-Father. Though I wonder if what that looks like has been distorted by years of performance-driven religion, shame-infused egoism, and our insatiable need to control one another. Fasting and prayer have a role in our spiritual lives that has been neglected by many, and there is nothing like self-sacrifice to keep the old ego in check; but, if that (all or any of the previous) were the key then we would be skipping meals, reciting more Scriptures and offering up prayers more regularly.

Some believe that it's a luck of the draw and a total act of the proverbial will of God, regardless of the people involved. "God chooses who He chooses. Nothing you can do about that."

Divine providence has been another way for us to say that God has favorites amongst his children, though we never admit to this consciously. It's a kind of apathetic fatalism that places the blame on God for a lack of manifestation of divinity in our lives. Unfortunately, this approach not only absolves us of responsibility but (even worse) creates in us a kind of spiritual inferiority complex. We come to believe that in some way we must be less than another child of God because God used, chose, or blessed them in a way that I want but never have experienced. This works-based approach either creates self-righteousness (if we perceive it working the way we want), or a deep sense of failure and condemnation for having "not done something right enough, long enough, good enough..." This party-line further entrenches in us the fundamental belief that we are not able to live as the Scriptures appear to instruct us to live. We are victims, doomed to fail, and forever limited by factors out of our control.

Strangely, our biblical examples didn't have the Bible, many worked demanding jobs, or simply were trying to survive under difficult circumstances and during perilous times. They were ordinary people, living ordinary lives, who did extraordinary things and experienced a kind of awakening that changed their lives (and the lives of others) in dramatic ways.

In this book the idea is to see merged some of those ancient experiences with modern ones. This in turn will bring to the surface some of the key ideas that our biblical examples leaned upon as they journeyed spiritually through their natural lives. Perhaps, when we get back to *the simplicity of the Gospel* we find our complications have buried the spiritual manifestations we have been longing for. Perhaps, we will find that it was not manifestations that we truly hungered for to begin with. Perhaps, we will even find something else. Something new. Something we never considered or even knew existed. Perhaps, if we lay aside our preconceived ideas and expectations of how we think life should go, we may find a whole new reality and way of living. Hebrews describes *"...by a new and living way, through the veil (which is his flesh)."* Rather than distancing ourselves from these ancient examples, perhaps we will see ourselves mirrored in them and they in us. The author of Hebrews (quoting the Psalms) wrote, "*Then said I, Lo, I come (in the volume of the book it is written of me,) to do thy will, O God.*" [Hebrews 10:20,7]

Let us begin the journey to find ourselves within the pages of the Book. Returning to the roots of what Jesus began thousands of years ago. His mission was clear; "*that all of them may be one, Father, just as you are in me and I am in you. May they also be in us so that the world may believe that you have sent me.*"

[John 17:21]

God Is Love

It takes great daring to open ourselves up to the possibility of a new way of being. There is great vulnerability in relinquishing our insatiable need for control. **Hebrews 10:20** eludes that a *"new and living way"* came through death on the cross. Often, we have to experience the death of the old to step into the new. Not that how things were or our past perspective was bad, but often we get so focused that we cannot see that growth and development requires change and flexibility. Since death is the ultimate surrender of control, we often fight or process the loss of control in the same way that we fight or process death. Change, like death, is inevitable. Only how we respond to it will determine the outcome of that change. I have learned that there are two options: we can fight it or we can work through it (process it).

There are many ways we fight change from ignoring and denying, to resisting and denigrating. All boil down to wrestling for a perceived loss of control. One way that we delude ourselves (fighting) into believing that we are in control (and often don't even recognize we are doing it) is with our beliefs about God and how He operates in our lives (and presumably in the lives of others). We call this *the walk of faith*, though I doubt much faith is involved since we dictate the terms (with phrases like: *"The Bible clearly says"*) and vehemently resist anything that would challenge our foundational beliefs. However, for true growth or transformation to occur, we must open ourselves up to the reality that we know very little when it comes to God and His workings in people. We only know what we see outwardly manifested by those who appear to be touched by God or highlighted in Scripture for our examples. How quickly we forget that what a person does with what God gives them is more of a reflection of the individual's spiritual state than God's seal of approval on their actions. King Saul went prophesying with the School of the Prophets while plotting to kill David out of jealousy and insecurity. [See 1 Samuel 19].

So, how are we to learn from these examples? I believe one vital step is to realize that we are not reading an example of the end goal, but rather are looking at an example of a journey. As with all voyages, it's important to know both the destination and the point of origin. God's original design set forth in Genesis was to create a being who was *His* image and likeness. We can begin from this point and attempt to move forward as we navigate the journey of discovery. What can we say other than *"God is Love*?" Not just any love, but all-encompassing, and selfless. Often, love is viewed from an emotional perspective, and a weak one at that. Of all the options, why would God choose such a vulnerable descriptor? The walk of love is the ultimate walk of faith since it requires a level of vulnerability that challenges even the most courageous of heroes.

What if our walk of faith is more like a lifelong love journey than a straight path to a clear destination? Not a marathon of arduous works and discipline or a stroll across the street of easy-peasy grace pleasing. What if it's more than steps, formulas, and strategies? This is truly transformational, because we like steps, formulas, and strategies. They give us that coveted sense of control and make us feel like we earned something based on our works/merit. We want to **earn** our value and prove our worth because it means we can use that standard to judge the worthiness of others and feel in control. Certainty is the most basic tool of our control-freak, ego-driven, world system.

What if we embraced a different reality? A redeemed back to The Garden view? How would our attitudes and perception of ourselves and others change? Paul declares to the people of Athens: "*'For in him we live and move and have our being.' As some of your own poets have said, 'We are his offspring'*". [Acts 17:28, NIV]. He did not speak this to the church, but rather as part of his evangelistic message. Paul declares to the Athenians: "We (that includes You, Athenians) are His offspring!" Paul included those yet to believe Athenians as already part of the family, the Body of Christ. This is *not* how evangelism is done today. I wonder if, and how, things would change if those seeking to *win* souls would stop telling people they are lost and start telling them they are loved. The people of Athens had made an idol to *The Unknown God*, and Paul used it as an opening, declaring who that Unknown God was. The Athenians were seekers, and God had been speaking to them all along, trying to reveal Himself, though they did not know it. It is religious pride to assume that God is not already speaking to all people just because those individuals do not embrace our way of relating to God.

This is the human condition, whether we are believers and followers of Christ or not: we long for mystery and are forever in search of the unknown. Here we find one of many lessons about the love of God for humanity: He uses your idols to tell you about Himself. Never forget it! God uses all of our idols. God's love is shameless. He will use whatever you are worshipping, serving, and degrading yourself with to show you Himself and teach you who you really are.

In our ego and need for control, we recognize that light or divine presence and proclaim (loud and proud): "See? I am right. My religion is right. My beliefs are *the truth*." All while clinging to that outward, hollow idol. We insist all others bend to our ways. In this way, God is made into just one more idol in our life. These idols have no life, and therefore are unknowable, hence the Unknown God. God, however, is all about knowing and being known. He is the relational God. From the beginning God is found walking with humanity.

First in the garden, and then with others. He walked with those like Enoch, Daniel, the three Hebrew children, David, Moses, Elijah, Jesus, the disciples, along with you and I.

I grew up in what is called *The Faith Movement*, and remember countless times hearing the "*if you have faith then* ...(insert action here)." This phrase would always preface whatever situation or circumstance needed changing or help. Although I doubt it was the original intent of the people who began the faith movement, somehow we have developed a sensationalized, transactional, self-serving, and impatient faith. If we don't get what we want quickly then we start in on the blame game. Looking for reasons why our faith didn't work. Desperate for someone or something to blame. **Why?** One reason is we are addicted to *control*. Few want to take the time and energy to walk with God (and each other, the more difficult of the two) in our humanity. The key here is the phrase; "*in our humanity.*"

Our humanity is that vulnerable, imperfect, and unpredictable (out of control) part of us that is susceptible to shame and insecure. Our humanity is what is grasping for value, worth, and control. It's not exciting, polished, or flashy to engage with God in our humanity, but that's exactly what God did in the Garden, and Jesus did with the disciples. It's messy, scary, and vulnerable. It feels much safer to revert to our self-preservation, self-gratification, and self-exaltation mechanism than to surrender in love and trust. This egoistic reaction of leaning toward blame rather than process goes all the way back to the Garden of Eden. Consider the following conversation;

> **God:** Adam, what have you done?
>
> **Adam:** It was that woman, YOU gave me God!
>
> **God:** Eve, what have you done?
>
> **Eve:** Yeah, the serpent tricked me, and I did it.

Kudos to Eve who owned up to her mistake! Usually we go the road of Adam and blame God for not coming through on His promises or setting us up to fail. We blame people for not obeying God so He could use them as instruments to bless us. We blame the devil. We blame ourselves for not doing, believing, confessing, or doing something enough to defeat the devil who was blocking our so-called blessings.

Blame is a dangerous game. Blame creates wedges between people in relationships, including our relationship with God. It stops growth, and artificially replaces the real answers we are seeking. It keeps us perpetual victims. with no recourse or hope of betterment. Blame is our favorite excuse for not growing both spiritually and emotionally. It is a distraction and an energy drain. We shift to blame when we do not know God, when we are unable to perceive Him in our present circumstance. Blame is an expression of the ego and is born out of fear and shame. Each of us have areas in which we need to be introduced to *The Unknown God*. The idol of uncertainty needs to be replaced with the introduction to an intimate life-producing relationship.

It is noteworthy that all the heroes of faith in the Bible had doubt, wavering, and failure-filled lives just like the rest of us. We tend to glaze over those parts. Yet, God still used them to part the Red Sea, deliver the people from captivity, conquer giants, and delivered the kingdom into their hands. These individuals had marital problems, anger management problems, and were liars, cheaters, and abusers of others. When we embrace all sides of these Bible Heroes, we can truly learn the deeper lessons being taught through their stories. If we truly embrace the whole story, then we must also accept that God can and will flow through our own failed lives with a message of life, hope, and restoration to those who witness our journey.

I believe the Bible still contains so many answers we have yet to discover. Our understanding of the truths therein are still growing, unfolding, and evolving. The Holy Spirit has been at work over the ages unravelling God's truths from our cultural bias and ego-bound natures. Our nationalism, patriotism, tribalism, racism, and other "isms" veil His true nature to us and through us. There is one ultimate truth, but I doubt any of us have understood it fully. Here's a place to start, and dare I say, where we will all conclude: God is Love. Most believers wholeheartedly believe that God is all-loving, all-knowing, and all-powerful; but, if we are honest with ourselves many of us believe God used flawed people in the Bible not because it pleased Him to do so, but because they were all He had to work with. Religion teaches us to believe that God merely tolerates humanity as a result of the spilled blood of Jesus. Friends, this is not love.

God is Love. Such a simple statement. Yet, each person will envision something different. To some this statement means *"God will give me what I want."* Essentially, God is a Sugar Daddy. Others will say it means God loves you too much to not punish you for the things you do that make Him angry: God is an impatient father. The Phrase *"God is Love"* could mean *"all the things in life that I like come from Him, but somehow He's not able or willing to stop the stuff I don't like. God is a limited and helpless parent, the victim of my shortcomings. God is Love could mean so many things!"*

Even in the Greek language, there are multiple words translated simply as *love*. There is friendly-brotherly love, a paternal-maternal love, an unconditional love, and a passionate-erotic love. Love is what we all seek yet no one can fully grasp. Most of us spend the majority of our time in a selfish kind of love. We love as long as it is comfortable for us. We love as long as it feels good, is beneficial, or aligns with our self-portrait. We use the pretext of love to consume one-another and fulfill our selfish desires. We treat love like a currency and talk about our *"love bank"*. We look to others in our lives and classify them as the fillers or emptiers of this love bank. Love is individual and entirely subjective both as an emotion and an idea. So, out of all the comparatives, why did God choose to identify Himself with Love?

For this precise reason, love is one of the best ideas we have for relating to God. Love must be experienced because it can never be completely understood or explained. Love graces, surprises, and flows outside of our ability to control it. Love burns like a raging, all-consuming fire, and love simmers and warms like a warm summer breeze. Love is multifaceted and multidimensional. Love connects hearts, minds, and souls. To quote Deon Jackson: *"Love makes the world go 'round"*. Love has both a stabilizing and destabilizing effect. Love can settle your wandering heart and at the same time turn your world on its ear, causing you to wander about in a stupor. Love is maddening and intoxicating. Love is life. **God is Love**.

Jesus told his disciples, *"Your love for one another will prove to the world that you are my disciples"* [John 13:35, NLT]. The proof of a follower of Christ is not their perfect moral lifestyle. It's not a perfect tithing record or church attendance. It's not miracles they work or produce. It's not hours in prayer and Bible study. The measure of a true disciple is love. Love for people. Love for the other. So, how is love seen and how is love known? Love can only be seen and known through experience. In order for someone to see this love there must be a connection, a relationship. This love we see in others is most often a projection of what we have within us. The byproducts of love are more easily seen: faithfulness, forgiveness, loyalty, mutuality, affection. All of these can be faked, and can come from a place other than love. All these can, as easily, come from fear and self-preservation. Love *must* be experienced to be known, just as God must be experienced to be known. To quote David, *"Taste and see that the Lord is good; blessed is the one who takes refuge in him"* [Psalms 34:8].

The love of God is a topic that deserves a book of its own; however, a few key verses of Scripture can open a small window into the kind of love by which Christlike faith works.

> **For in Jesus Christ neither circumcision availeth anything, nor uncircumcision; but faith which worketh by love.**
> [Galatians 5:6]

Love renders works and shallow efforts obsolete. If it does not find it's origins in love, then it is not faith. The Book of James states *"faith without works is dead"*. Still, the foundation of our faith (and the works that accompany it) must be love, or else we are not true to the One from *and* in whom our faith flows.

Love is part of a holy trinity along with hope and faith. Faith, Hope, and Love are not a tight, exclusive circle, but rather are an open round inviting all who will to come join them. Through intimacy, vulnerability, and trust these create, renew, and restore *life in the Garden*. In 1 Corinthians we are told, *"Three things will last forever - faith, hope, and love - and the greatest of these is love"*. Love must be the plumb line and our guiding source for any endeavor of faith and any matter of hope. Because of God's great love for us He sent His Son to walk among us, as us.

Love made heaven uncomfortable if we were to be absent from it. If we are to reflect (walk out) the same kind of love that God has for us to a lost and dying humanity (both inside and outside the "church"), we must experience that love ourselves. We must know it, feel it, and see it as irrefutable truth. It must become a part of us, as real and close as our very breath. God's love must be as tangible as the atmosphere we live in. The best any of us can do is to offer imperfect examples (stories and allegories), and hope that in the shared experience we may begin to perceive Love and experience Love for ourselves.

I have read a section from 1 Corinthians for decades. It was only recently I began to think of the love chapter as more than a challenge for me to grow in my own love life. Sometimes we get it backwards. I realized one day, that I cannot give what I have not received. If I am to love unconditionally I must first receive unconditional love and allow myself to both accept and experience it. The following gives us a working definition of this unconditional love, a starting place for understanding the character of God.

Love is patient and kind. Love is not jealous or boastful or proud or rude. It does not demand its own way. It is not irritable, and it keeps no record of being wronged. It does not rejoice about injustice but rejoices whenever the truth wins out. Love never gives up, never loses faith, is always hopeful, and endures through every circumstance.
[I Corinthians 13:4-7, NLT]

Since God is love, these verses also tell us a bit about God-qualities along with love-qualities. Where you see the word love (*agapeo* in the Greek) insert God. God is patient and kind. So, put away from you the image of a grumpy old guy just waiting for you to screw up! God is not jealous or boastful or proud. Let it sink in! What? God is not jealous? No, we are, but He is not. God is not rude either. God does *not* rejoice about injustice, but whenever truth wins out. God never gives up. God never loses faith. He is always hopeful and endures (outlasts) every circumstance. God does not demand His own way! God never loses faith in you! He is ever hopeful of you! God outlasts every circumstance. *Every. Single. One.* Be it the ones you created by ignorance and selfish decisions. God outlasts every circumstance thrust upon you; whether you were aware of it or not. Drink in the following passage, and take it personally, as it was meant to be:

What then shall we say to these things? If God is for us, who is against us? He who did not spare His own Son, but delivered Him over for us all, how will He not also with Him freely give us all things? Who will bring a charge against God's elect? God is the one who justifies who is the one who condemns? Christ Jesus is He who died, yes, rather who was raised, who is at the right hand of God, who also intercedes for us. Who will separate us from the love of Christ? Will tribulation, or distress, or persecution, or famine, or nakedness, or peril, or sword? Just as it is written,

"FOR YOUR SAKE WE ARE BEING PUT TO DEATH ALL DAY LONG; WE WERE CONSIDERED AS SHEEP TO BE SLAUGHTERED."

But in all these things we overwhelmingly conquer through Him who loved us. For I am convinced that neither death, nor life, nor angels, nor principalities, nor things present, nor things to come, nor powers, nor height, nor depth, nor any other created thing, will be able to separate us from the love of God, which is in Christ Jesus our Lord.
[Romans 8:31-39, *NASB*]

When we truly perceive that absolutely nothing will separate us from God's love, and that His love has no hint of selfishness or self-serving qualities, then we will begin to be empowered to love others in the same way. This was the love that empowered Jesus to proclaim from the cross: "Father forgive them, they know not what they do!" First, Jesus had to experience the Father loving him (as a man) in this way. In The Book of John, Jesus says to His disciples: "As the Father has loved me, so have I loved you. Now remain in my love." Our challenge is *to remain* in His love. Jesus grew up for most of his life without a natural father (Joseph died when Jesus was young. Being the natural oldest of Mary's sons, he took over Joseph's obligations per Jewish custom). Jesus learned early on to rely on his Heavenly Father to fill that void and heal the wound of abandonment.

Take a moment. Right now, close your eyes, and find your sacred, secret, inner sanctuary. Ask the Father to reveal to you His love. Allow that love to wash over you, fill you, and heal your inner person. Go back and reread the previous verses from a new point of view. Not by an Old Testament, religious, performance obsessed god. But by the point of view of one loved by God as is described in First Corinthians 13.

Life Is Motion

As we embark on this journey of laying aside everything we think we know, having the foundation of LOVE is essential because growth is messy. As it says in Ephesians *"Then Christ will make his home in your hearts as you trust in him. Your roots will grow down into God's love and keep you strong."* [Ephesians 3:17, NLT] Here the best I can do is share some of my own journey, and then follow it with some biblical examples that have spoken to and inspired me.

I'm somewhat of an enigma in that I am such an extroverted, people-person and yet in my gifting and spiritual life I am called to a great deal of solitude. Sometimes that translates into loneliness and a sense of a lack of meaningful connection with others. Regardless, I crave solitude. I'm drawn to it like a moth to the flame. When no one else is around, a place inside me comes alive and I'm awakened to the truth inside of me. However, when I emerge from my solitude all I want is to connect with others. What I glean from those deep, quiet places has more meaning when I can share it with others. This is partly because I process better talking with others than simply mulling it over on the inside. I used to interpret my need for connection with a need for approval.

I would chastise and berate myself as proud and selfish. Why do we run from that which gives us life? Why do we demonize that which brings us joy? I'm learning not to run from solitude, and not to demonize my need for meaningful connections. I'm finding such sweetness in solitude: no one around, but my God and His creation.

Ironically, it's in being alone that I am most aware that I am never truly alone. Not only will He never leave or forsake me, but I have been immersed into the Body of Christ. My connection to humanity is unavoidable. I'm learning to consciously connect with those who appreciate me for who I am, and embrace my higher connection with all of humanity.

As I was out on a walk at the beginning of summer I was enjoying the quiet solitude of my favorite nature trail. It had just rained a few hours earlier and everything was still damp, green, and vibrantly alive. There is something about the smell of nature just after a good rain. Like the trees and lush greenery that surrounded me, I too was drinking in the refreshing effects of the damp air. One thing that I appreciate about winter is how much it increases my enjoyment of spring and summer. Like fasting, winter has a way of cleansing and resetting us so we both appreciate and do not miss the blessed refreshing of spring, the growth of summer, and the fruit of autumn.

As I walked in the quiet, I noticed the rustling of the leaves and branches in the breeze, birds flitting about, and a rabbit making a mad dash away from my path. Life is never truly still. Our world really is not a quiet one. I focused on the beauty around me and felt the damp air hydrating my skin, filling my lungs, and refreshing my soul. *"As a deer longs for flowing streams, so I long for you, God."* [Psalms 42:1, CSB]

God often speaks to me in parallels or connections. As I walked physically I pondered my spiritual walk. We were meant to walk the path of righteousness. When Jesus invited people to become his disciples, he said: Come, and follow me. There is a certain degree of leaving that needs to happen to follow. I have heard His call to follow me on many occasions. First, the call to awaken to my salvation: I was drawn to the altars at the tender age of 3, and then again six months later to receive the baptism of the Holy Spirit. There have been so many other callings: moving from Costa Rica to Lake City, Michigan, helping this church, engaging in missions work, marrying my husband, moving to this city and that. Missions trips to Panama, Mexico, Costa Rica, and Argentina. It struck me how even the revelations of the Spirit are ever in motion.

Follow Me. Walk with Me. Leaving the familiar to move in the direction of the unknown, new believing, and new living. "Follow Me" requires growing, evolving, changing, and becoming more. Not everything we leave behind is bad. Our religious minds try to boil everything down to good and bad, right and wrong. In reality, our journey of faith has nothing to do with good and bad, right and wrong. In Second Corinthians, Paul describes our progression in Christ as going from glory to glory. [see Chapter 3 verse 18]

Often we leave behind fruitful, healthy things simply because they are not part of what is needed for the next segment of the journey. As in the fall, trees drop their leaves in anticipation of winter, sometimes the call to "follow me" requires us to let go of the very things that have been feeding, covering, and fueling us. Like leaves on a tree, they slowly cease to function, fade, and eventually fall away. That can be scary and confusing. Our job is to recognize the season and embrace it.

Our tendency is to cling to a static, unchanging truth. I wonder why we fight growth so much since it is such an integral part of even our natural existence? Science has shown that we humans don't start dying until we stop growing. Our egoistic need for control may be a big part of this tendency. Western culture doesn't help either. When something that was fruitful stops bearing fruit, our tendency is to jump to shame, blame, and judgement. Everything changes. Perhaps not the original intent, but at least in our understanding or interpretation. Like the aforementioned tree, new leaves will grow in the spring.

I continued to walk and pray, I meditated and pondered on the truths, principles, and revelations that I have brought with me into my present. Like the roots of a tree, they run deep, grounding and stabilizing me. Some are visible from the surface, branching outward and connecting to others. Others are hidden beneath the surface, running deep into my soul, and imprinting on the very fabric of my identity. I'm not talking about believing God for money or even healing. Those are basic, superficial aspects of faith. Like fruit on a tree, they grow back every year and are consumables. I'm talking about those truths that I believe about myself, God, and the way "things" work (reality as I perceive it). My natural and spiritual world-view. Especially when I used to believe a lie, but now it's replaced with truth.

I used to believe that if I did all the right things: pray, fast, study my Bible daily, tithe, and confess the Word that any problems I met would be conquered quickly so I could return to my "life of ease, err, I mean, faith." Then life happened. I've learned that everything isn't dependent on my works; however, it can be (to a certain degree) if I want it to. That being said, I'm not consistent enough, perfect enough, and undoubting enough to measure up to my own standards.

I'm so glad that God has me on a better journey. A journey of discovering who I already am. A journey of discovering who He is. The One who has always loved me. I still pray, fast, study, give, and all those other things. Though I'll admit that the way I do them has evolved over the years, and my motivation is quite different.

The biggest and most important difference I have realized is that my "why" has evolved, or matured if you prefer. I do all these things because of love. I do because it's who I am. The disciplines I engage in are not boxes of to-do's to check off, but tools for unlocking or discovering my God-identity. Like a bird that sings, a frog that croaks, or a lion that roars. I do me. When I forget, run out of time, or get distracted and don't "do one (or all) of my do's" I don't feel bad. I do not pray, study, fast, give, or anything else out of obligation, fear, or to feel worthy. This is freedom, life, and unconditional love. My Creator loves me whether I recognize it or not. He loves all humanity regardless of her response.

It hit me on that walk that the truly lasting, impactful, and effective "Gospel Truths" that have endured the test of time are the ones that I have lived. I've walked them out and lived, breathed, and had my being in them. The fads fade. Only what is real remains. One of these truths is: Life is Motion.

Although I serve a God "Who changes not" I and the world around me are in a constant state of change. Change does not bother God. If I let it, if I cooperate with God, and if I will be brave enough to let go, change is my vehicle forward. To quote Robbie Sharma:"Change is hard at first, messy in the middle, and gorgeous at the end." When God created time, He set into motion days, weeks, months, years and the seasons that we experience in the natural world. He didn't have to do it that way. God could have created a natural world that was temperate all over without seasons. We could have had multiple suns so that there would never be (what we experience as) night.

The Holy Spirit spoke this to me one morning as I was waking from a dream: "You carry the light and revelation of the Lord's year. Not a year as in a number of days, but a year as in a cycle of seasons that repeats (winter, spring, summer, fall). A year as in a growing process with times of rest, new life, growth, and letting go of what is no longer necessary to make room for new life after another season of rest. Not a year or cycle of fear, destruction, and woe. A "year" or cycle of love, light, and unity to grow. For you know the Shepherd and you know His voice."

The following chart is will help clarify the connection between the natural seasons and some of their spiritual significance;

The Natural	The Spiritual
Winter	Rest. No outward signs of productivity. Preparation for a new cycle of producing life. Internal, sometimes wordless formation of vision. Early stages of pregnancy.
Spring	Marked with refreshing and the early signs of new life. Evidence of something new coming. Pregnancy evident to all who have eyes to see.
Summer	Birth, growth, and productivity. The vision is formed and can be seen and expressed. Outward signs of fruit, some but not all mature.
Fall	Peak of fruitful, harvesting season. Toward the end, leaves begin to fade, wilt, and fall. Can have a "smell of dying" just before Winter sets in.

Another truth: **God loves me unconditionally, no matter what.** I'm secure in His love because there is nothing I can do or not do that He doesn't already know about, and for which He does not already have a plan. I cannot surprise God. I am also not so powerful that I can mess up His plans beyond repair. Third: It will take my entire lifetime to even scratch the surface of knowing God and His love for me. I will have false beliefs that He will challenge, and I will stumble in the dark at times. This knowledge keeps me humble, teachable, and always ready to learn and grow. It also helps me to fight the urge to judge others, because we are all in the same boat. It's worth it now and will all be worth it in the end. Finally, God is with me. There is no place He won't go with me. I am **never** alone. Although I believe and study many other things, the previous statements have been fundamental to my journey of faith. They ground me, keep me real, and comfort my heart when I wrestle with the many questions I have and circumstances I don't understand.

This walk of faith, hope, and love is a journey. Although we serve a God who changes not, we are ever growing in our capacity for perceiving and experiencing God.

Instead of viewing our growth from a negative perspective of "ridding ourselves of the bad stuff," consider the perspective offered to us here; *"We all, with unveiled faces, are looking as in a mirror at the glory of the Lord and are being transformed into the same image from glory to glory; this is from the Lord who is the Spirit."* [2 Corinthians 3:18, CSB]. Consider that the yearly cycle of seasons is there for our benefit. When all seems "dead, barren, and fruitless," I have not failed God. I am not abandoned or cursed. It is winter. Rest, settle in, allow the unseen to incubate, develop, and form within you.

A very vivid example of the unveiling, mentioned in Second Corinthians passage above, is found in the Gospel of Luke, Two disciples were journeying on the road to Emmaus after the crucifixion, when the resurrected Jesus comes alongside them and inserts Himself into their conversation. Following is a section of that conversation:

He said to them, "How foolish you are, and how slow to believe all that the prophets have spoken! Did not the Messiah have to suffer these things and then enter his glory?" And beginning with Moses and all the Prophets, he explained to them what was said in all the Scriptures concerning himself. As they approached the village to which they were going, Jesus continued on as if he were going farther. But they urged him strongly, "Stay with us, for it is nearly evening; the day is almost over." So he went in to stay with them. When he was at the table with them, he took bread, gave thanks, broke it and began to give it to them. Then their eyes were opened and they recognized him, and he disappeared from their sight. They asked each other, "Were not our hearts burning within us while he talked with us on the road and opened the Scriptures to us?"
[Luke 24:25-32 NIV]

God is still inserting Himself into the conversation of our journey. Talking, walking, and teaching us through life's moments: both difficult and joyous. God is about the business of revealing His love to us, so that we may see His love in us, and then show His Love to others.

When we have met with Him on the road with open eyes and hearts the result will be that our hearts will burn within us while He talks and opens the Scriptures to us. Like the two disciples, it is in the breaking of bread, the relationship, that our eyes are open and we recognize Jesus for Who He is. Jesus sealed the revelation that the disciples were receiving with relationship. He stopped the motion long enough for them to perceive Him and recognize the depth and significance of this moment. Once they recognized Him, they also found themselves (His image and likeness) at which point they became Jesus to the world and a separate Jesus was no longer needed.

Although God's presence is always with us, these moments when we become keenly aware are times when revelation and relationship take a plunge into the depths of our souls. In these moments we who are normally spiritually incoherent become lucid. We awaken to the realities that we somehow always knew but were not consciously aware. Something resonates within us, and from the depths of our beings there is a resounding YES! In those moments we fulfill the scripture *"In this [union and fellowship with Him], love is completed and perfected with us, so that we may have confidence in the day of judgment [with assurance and boldness to face Him]; because as He is, so are we in this world."* [1 John 4:17, AMP].

I remember one such moment of lucidity. I was worshipping God on a Sunday like any other. As is my custom, I had stopped singing along with the words in the songs and instead was singing in the Spirit. Suddenly I became aware of my connection first to God, then to the believers in the room, and then to those throughout the world. I felt the blood coursing through my veins, and knew that it represented the spiritual blood that unites us through Christ. The following scripture rose up in my spirit:

> For this reason I bow my knees before the Father from whom every family in heaven and on earth derives its name, that He would grant you, according to the riches of His glory, to be strengthened with power through His Spirit in the inner man so that Christ may dwell in your hearts through faith; and that you, being rooted and grounded in love, may be able to comprehend with all the saints what is the breadth and length and height and depth, and to know the love of Christ which surpasses knowledge, that you may be filled up to all the fullness of God. Now to Him who is able to do far more abundantly beyond all that we ask or think, according to the power that works within us, to Him be the glory in the church and in Christ Jesus to all generations forever and ever. Amen.
> [Ephesians 3:14-21, NASB]

I had often prayed these very verses over the years. This time, however, the revelation of the significance hit me like a ton of bricks: "in heaven and on earth." I'm not just connected to the saints living, but those who have passed as well. So are you! All the greats. I draw my strength, energy, and spiritual power from a deep and ancient source.

Biblical and historical brothers and sisters in Christ, whether you knew them personally or not, are your heritage. All are one in Christ. Physical death does not diminish the Body of Christ. The disciples on the road to Emmaus were grieving because of their belief that they had been "separated" from Jesus. They believed that they had "lost" Him forever and would be left living without the comfort of His presence and the benefits of His wisdom. Not too many years before this experience I had lost my father. Not only was he my natural father, but he was also my mentor and a great source of encouragement, comfort, and wisdom. In that moment I realized not just doctrinally or theoretically, but experientially, that nothing is ever lost.

All the wisdom, comfort, and encouragement is still here…in Christ. Every bit of God that was revealed in him is still in Christ. Since that time, I have experienced the flavor of God that was my earthly father in various people. It blesses my heart, encourages my soul, and enriches me spiritually. Though the natural vessel changes, the reflection of The Father is the same.

Why not pause right now? Close your eyes and enter into your secret place with your Heavenly Father. Reach out with your spiritual senses and connect to your Heavenly family. Regardless of your natural race, heritage, or background you have a rich, ancient, and diverse heritage from which to draw strength. Allow the Holy Spirit to unite you with Heaven's host and ask the Lord what he would like to impart into you today for the journey ahead. If you feel alone, separate, or abandoned, allow the fellowship of the spirit to heal your heart and dissolve your loneliness.

Stranger in a Strange Land

I remember as a young teen the first time I read in Genesis where God told Abram to "go to a place that I will show you." I too could hear the voice of God calling me into the unknown. At the time, I lived with my parents on the mission field in Costa Rica. Other missionary kids would talk about their parents' call to missions as a burden or annoyance that they had to tolerate. These young people lived for the times they could return "home to the States." Some rebelled and made life difficult for their parents. I saw my parent's assignment as our family's call. Even though when the decision was made I was too young to be a part of making it, I was part of that vision and that vision was a part of me. I had this inner knowing that God had a purpose for me in the "here and now." I knew that I had a purpose born of God regardless of my physical location. How could it be otherwise? Over the years I have continued to identify with Abraham. No matter where I live I have the sense that I am a "stranger in a strange land." Always either out of time or place. Never quite belonging or fitting in, yet called for purpose.

I wonder if Abram and Sarai had the same or similar feelings? By the time we get to their story in Genesis, Abram and Sarai should have been raising a family (like all the other happy, respectable couples their age). More than likely, they would have had grandchildren! Abram was well acquainted with sacrifices, offerings, and spiritual disciplines. Doubtless he and Sarai had done all that they could to secure the ability to bear children. After years of being in his religious system, nothing had worked for Abram and Sarai. Their heart's desire to have a child remained unfulfilled. None of the spiritual disciplines or usual processes that they thought were vital for "victory" were working. Perhaps it was not meant to be?

Just before I turned eighteen, I felt God calling me to move out of my parents' house, off the mission field that I loved, and to Michigan (Lake City) to attend college and begin my adult journey. I knew that I would not marry a Costa Rican man and that God had purpose for me in the United States. I had no idea what that purpose was exactly; however, I had been raised to be comfortable with uncertainty and the unknown, and to be an independent, risk-taker. One thing I was certain of is that ministry, most certainly missions was in my future. It was in my blood. What I found awaiting me was nothing like what I expected or imagined. From weather to culture to how church operates, this Northern Michigan City was a strange land indeed!

As the preacher-missionary daughter, I was used to being "in the know." Opportunities to be involved in ministry were plentiful. I was accustomed to being involved, included in a family, having a voice, and in leadership positions where appropriate. I was valued and trusted. In this new place I was "a stranger in a strange land." No one was unkind per se. I just did not belong. My voice and opinion didn't matter. What I had to say on the matter was not wanted. I was not "known" so I was not trusted. I found myself wandering in a wilderness of disconnection, offense, rejection, and isolation for many years looking for "a city whose builder and maker is God." God was pointing me down a very different path than that of my parents.

God's journey for Abraham pointed him down a different path as well. Rather than perfection, sacrifice, and holiness, the story of Abraham is about belief (trust), hope, and a reshaped identity. When God called Abram out of Ur of the Chaldeas he said, "Come to a land that I will show you." No details. No GPS. Just blindly follow. Day by day. Step by step. This is why he is called *The Father of Faith*. Not because he did everything right, but because he trusted the God who makes everything right. This was and continues to be my journey: a journey that trusts that even when things don't seem right, I am following the God who makes it all right. When I doubt, when I fail, when I just have no clue, I trust that He has it all in hand and I keep walking. Often this walking feels more like free-falling. It is not a sensational, Hollywood, glamorous walk of faith. It's messy. It's scary. It's beautiful. It's slow, tedious, and at times lonely. Such was the journey of Abraham and Sarah. The Book of Hebrews relays the following:

> **By faith Abraham, when he was called to go out into a place which he should after receive for an inheritance, obeyed; and he went out, not knowing whither he went. By faith he sojourned in the land of promise, as in a strange country, dwelling in tabernacles with Isaac and Jacob, the heirs with him of the same promise: For he looked for a city which hath foundations, whose builder and maker is God. Through faith also Sara herself received strength to conceive seed, and was delivered of a child when she was past age, because she judged him faithful who had promised…(Of whom the world was not worthy:) they wandered in deserts, and in mountains, and in dens and caves of the earth.**
> [Hebrews 11:8-11, 38]

God has been known to call his chosen ones out to desert and wilderness places. Joseph's pit that his brothers threw him in was in the wilderness [Genesis 37:22]. God called the children of Israel out of Egypt and into the wilderness (a three day journey) to meet with Him [Exodus 3:18]. Later In Exodus [13:18] it says that God lead the people (to the promised land) through the way of the wilderness. The Hebrew word used for way (*darak*) means a road, journey, or way of life. When being called out of what is known and familiar into the new and unfamiliar (for which we have no frame of reference or experience) God uses this "way of the wilderness" to lead us.

David, who was called to be a different kind of king, spent much time in solitude tending his father's flock in the wilderness, not to mention his years of running from Saul. Before beginning His ministry, Jesus was drawn into the desert by the Holy Spirit. When Jesus wanted to spend time with his close disciples to teach them, He would pull them aside. Paul spent years on his backside of the desert to gain his revelation of grace. If you find yourself in a desert place or in the wilderness, consider that you may be on the wilderness way of God.

The Holy Spirit has you on a journey to deliver Egypt out of you so that you can fully enter the Land of Promise. The Egyptian way of life was a system that used slavery to fuel its economy. It was a system in which those of power and status were valued and those lacking power or status were only valued for what they could do for the "rich and powerful." This Egypt-system returned in Roman times and is very much in place today as well. It takes a certain amount of isolation and soul-fasting to detox from this consumerist and egocentric way of living.

Consider each of the examples: Abram (and Sarai), Joseph, the children of Israel, David, Jesus and His disciples. All these examples (and many more) were tried, challenged, and faced both victories and defeats on the way to the realization of God's promises. Each one had to leave behind the familiar and learn to embrace the unfamiliar and the unknown. They had to relinquish consumerism, control, and self preservation to enter into a "new and living way."

What is God calling you out of so that He can bring you into a fuller manifestation of His divine identity for you? Are you clinging to a place, idea, or way of doing and being? Only you can chose to embrace the way of the wilderness and allow the solitude and the stripping away of all that is familiar (the spiritual fall season) to open space for you to conceive (the spiritual winter season) and grow (spring and summer) God's purpose and plan for your life, family, and ministry.

Take time today and everyday to get quiet and listen to the still small voice of the Spirit, guiding and leading you on paths of righteousness. Ask the Lord: "Help me to identify what season I am in. What would you tell me today? How would you lead me? What false beliefs or things of the past do I need to let go of so that I can embrace more of my identity in You?"

First Things First

As I walked my favorite nature hike path one solitary, isolated, spring day, I continued to ponder my connection to Abraham. I quickened my pace and felt the resistance of the wind pushing back against my advance. **Isaiah 40:31** rose up in my spirit: *"They that wait upon the Lord shall renew their strength…"* My energy returned as I focused on my own vision, the desires and longings of my heart. My heart for missions and the nations has not abated over the years. My idea of how God can use me has been adjusted. I used to think the only way to do missions was to raise money and move to the country to which you were called. I'm certain I have missed so many opportunities here in the United States while God was teaching me missions is all around me, because it is in me. I'm thankful for the lessons I learned through Abraham. I no longer feel regret or guilt at the realization my "missed" opportunities were no surprise to God. They form part of my own wilderness way and served to strip me of the familiar to build God's real and true purpose for my life.

My journey, like Abraham & Sarah's has not been without its trials, failings, and challenges. I rehearsed one of my life verses *"For we are his workmanship, created in Christ Jesus for good works, which God prepared beforehand, that we should walk in them."* [Ephesians 2:10, ESV]. I remembered I also have a unique path laid before me with precision and care. I shake off the temptation to play the "what if?" game that leads to feelings of regret, and embrace a more relevant truth: *"For it is God which worketh in you both to will and to do of his good pleasure."* [Philippians 2:13]. Each step, whether a stride or a stumble, brings me closer to the manifestation of what my heart already sees and knows to be true, real, and present. This is our heritage of faith that conquers hopeless situations: *"He who began a good work in us will complete it."* [Philippians 1:6, ESV]. I have sure and precious promises from my Father who loves me. He gives me both the desires of my heart and the desires in my heart. What's more, since He is my creator, everything I need to fulfill my purpose comes built in! I fail only when I forget who I am, but no failure is final. When I remember who I am, I can arise and continue my journey. Every failure serves to reveal an area where I am confused about my true identity and serves to reveal more of Christ in me! Why? Because God is love, and love never fails. **Love is the ultimate last man standing.**

Love is first. After that all will follow. The Apostle John said *"There is no fear in love; but perfect love casteth out fear: because fear hath torment. He that feareth is not made perfect in love"* [1 John 4:18]. Every problem I've ever had has essentially boiled down to a love problem. This is a truth that has been years in the making for me. I used to believe that faith and hard work were the ingredients to a successful Christian life. Have a character problem? Pray, read the Word, and use your faith! Have a financial problem? Pray, read the Word, and use your faith! In need of healing or you name it? Pray, read the Word, and use your faith! For ministry to be successful (whatever that means), I must have faith (a.k.a. take risks) and work hard. If God was truly in it, then it will succeed and I will prosper (become popular, gain the financial support to do the work, etc.). If God is not in it then it doesn't matter what I do, it's not going to work.

Not only is this line of thinking illogical and unbiblical, it is also cruel. It is cruel because every so-called set back translates into me somehow being not enough and a failure

as both a believer and a child of God. This line of thinking (or something similar to it) is deeply rooted in the Christian Religion. Note, I did not say *Christianity*. Christ-followers live from a redeemed position that is not based on works we have done, but on what Christ has done for us: God so LOVED the world that He gave His only begotten Son. That pattern was foreshadowed (in seed form) with Abraham and Sarah:
"Therefore, the promise comes by faith, so that it may be by grace and may be guaranteed to all Abraham's offspring--not only to those who are of the law but also to those who have the faith of Abraham. He is the father of us all." [Romans 4:16].

If we examine Abraham's faith, it was relational. His faith was based on trust. Abraham's faith was neither ritualistic nor legalistic. His covenant cutting ritual was a common pagan practice. When done from a place of trust, faith, and love, there really isn't much God cannot or will not work with. According to Hebrews Sarah received strength to conceive (and survive childbirth at her age) because she judged Him faithful Who had promised. Other Bible translations have used the word *considered* instead of judged, which seems a little more palatable. The fact is Sarah had to make a judgement about God's character to receive or reject the promise and walk out the natural process.

Regardless of the semantics, whether you say deem, consider, or judge, Sarah made a decision about the nature of God's character. Whether we are brave enough to admit it or not, we too are making decisions about the nature of God's character on a daily basis. Often our actions (or inaction) show us best how we have judged God. Sarah did not start off just trusting God was faithful. She walked the journey with Abraham. She was delivered unscathed from the Egyptian king's hands after her husband (out of fear) lied about their relationship and gave her away. She received her husband back unharmed from wars and famines and countless other perils. For Sarah, what began with a laugh ended in the successful delivery of the promised child.

Sometimes, starting is the hardest part of the journey. Getting that initial momentum to break the atrophy that has set in from idle waiting can be so foreign. Breaking through the barrier of indecision can also be a difficult thing. What if I start out in the wrong direction? I'm certain that Abram and Sarai were no strangers to the fear of failure. Where did God start with Abraham and Sarah (Abram & Sarai at the time)? Before they ever realized it, Abram and Sarai were designed to reflect the image and likeness of the Creator. We know this as we look on from the future and read their story. They were to be "fruitful, multiply, and fill the earth" as it says in Genesis.

Before they were even aware of His existence, **YWVH** (Existing) put into motion a plan to draw out of Abram and Sarai the reflected image and likeness within them. In order for Abraham to become that faith model for a different way, a way that was not earned by works, he (and Sarah) had to get there without works. The journey, as for so many of us, began with emptiness. There was a void in their lives. A lack. A longing. Sounds like the Creation Story? They desired to have a child. To bring forth life. To leave a heritage. To nurture, and love, and be nurtured and loved. As usual, God's desire for them was much greater than their desire for themselves. Their desire was for a child, but God's was for a People.

Nevertheless, God used their small desire to bring forth His greater desire which was "beyond what they could ask or think." Like the boy's five loaves and two fish Jesus used to feed a multitude, God would take their natural desire to preserve a single family and use it to preserve a nation of people. None of their works could get them there because their purpose was to become a conduit of faith for living a different way. This way of *being* was so foreign to Abraham and Sarah, as it is to so many of us, that God had to take them on a journey through a process of total identity transformation. It was a long and messy journey, just like yours and mine. As the saying goes: "The journey of a thousand miles begins with a single step." Abraham and Sarah had to start. They had to get off of the status quo path, and enter that arena of the walk of faith. To quote Theodore Roosevelt:

> *"It is not the critic who counts; not the man who points out how the strong man stumbles, or where the doer of deeds could have done them better. The credit belongs to the man who is actually in the arena, whose face is marred by dust and sweat and blood; who strives valiantly; who errs, who comes short again and again, because there is no effort without error and shortcoming; but who does actually strive to do the deeds; who knows great enthusiasms, the great devotions; who spends himself in a worthy cause; who at the best knows in the end the triumph of high achievement, and who at the worst, if he fails, at least fails while daring greatly, so that his place shall never be with those cold and timid souls who neither know victory nor defeat."*

Now unto him that is able to do exceeding abundantly above all that we ask or think, according to the power that worketh in us.
[Ephesians 3:20]

Could it be that God is desirous to take your small desire and use it to do exceedingly abundantly above all you could ask or think?

There is a pattern in Scripture of God choosing unlikely candidates to fulfill His divine purposes. A barren couple to produce a nation certainly qualifies. So does a poor shepherd boy, son of a concubine to be the King of a nation? How about a young girl forced into an arranged marriage to save a nation? Whatever He has called and purposed you for, you may feel like He chose the wrong person. David, Esther, Moses, and many others felt the same way. Don't allow your own perceived limitations to keep you from dreaming the dream and pursuing the vision. The Word of the Lord to me concerning God's plans for this season in the Body of Christ is.

> *"The Glory of the Bride will again come from those who are ordinary: the fisherman, the postal worker, the store clerk, the housekeeper, and the student. The lawyer, the school teacher, the highway patrol. Both the overlooked and unexpected will come into the light with direction and revelation that is revolutionary and out of sight. The fresh and the revolutionary is not in a pulpit or on a television screen. Don't look to the "known," the famous, and usual. It is found in the hearts, minds, souls, hands of the ones on the streets. Fishers of men, even tax collectors, ordinary folk, like Jesus' disciples of old. You are hearing "Come, follow Me!"*

Take some time to explore your desires. Write them down and choose one to focus on in prayer. Ask God to expand your vision and reveal His desires for you. Ask Him to show you a different perspective of the obstacles and struggles that you have been meeting with on your journey toward your Promised Land. What false beliefs, traditions, or religious views is He attempting to uproot from your heart? Let them go. Dare greatly to embrace the truths about yourself and your purpose that He is revealing to you today.

A New Name

The journey of faith and hope often takes us to places we never dreamed possible and often did not consider. To quote a friend and mentor: "Sometimes you don't know what you don't know." The author of Romans puts it this way:

> **In the same way, the Spirit helps us in our weakness. We do not know what we ought to pray for, but the Spirit himself intercedes for us through wordless groans. And he who searches our hearts knows the mind of the Spirit, because the Spirit intercedes for God's people according to the will of God."**
> [Romans 8:26-27, NIV]

Herein lies the mysterious work of the Holy Spirit in our lives: working out from beneath the layers those hidden truths we didn't know to ask about. Our divine identity is concealed by layers of culture, lies, and religious dogma. All of us. Not one of us has fully unveiled the glory that lies within our earthen vessels. Plenteous are the voices that tell us we cannot, are not, or should not. Many are the reasons why we have no right to dream a dream and pursue a purpose. So it is often still necessary for God to go straight to the foundations of identity as He did with Abraham and Sarah. He changed their names. When God changed Abram's name to Abraham, He made a public statement that he would be the father of many nations of the earth. *"No longer will you be called Abram; your name will be Abraham, for I have made you a father of many nations."* [Genesis 17:5 NIV]. This journey had many aspects, but here we will look at identity from the perspective of the changing of their names.

Most of Abram's ancestors were already fathers by the time that they had turned 30 or 35; yet Terah (Abram's father) was seventy years old before he had Abram. Abram's name suggests that Terah acknowledged that he could not claim parenthood of this son as his own achievement. Abram means he was fathered from above [see Genesis 11:12-26]. Even though Terah worshipped other gods, he knew that his son's existence came about in extraordinary circumstances and named him accordingly. One reason I relate to Abraham is because mine was also a miraculous birth. Although my parents were not in their 70's, my birth had complications which could have ended up at best in an emergency C-section and at worst in my (and possibly my mom's) death. After much prayer, and just before rushing my mom to surgery, I was born feet first (the worst kind of breech birth possible). Like Abram, I come from a heritage that knows the power of God in desperate situations. Abram had precedence for believing he (and Sarai) could have children at age seventy; however, Abram was *seventy-five* before God appeared to him, changed his name, and promised to make him a "father of many nations." As the one fathered from above, Abram could have just assumed that by virtue of his own specialness he and Sarai could produce after their own kind. He would just be carrying on his own father's legacy, right? Yes, and no.

My father used to always tell me that a good father, pastor, or mentor never wants his children to start where he started. "A true father wants his children to stand on his shoulders and go higher and farther than the father was able to go. With his dying breath he should be thrusting the next generation forward, armed with all the resources of the past generation." Heritage is to be carried forward, not discarded to start over. Yes, some things may change or even be let go of, but this should not be done lightly.

Abram had a heritage of trusting in the divine to bring forth fruit in old age. Just as God used part of Abram's (and Sarai's) name in their new names to build upon it, he was to use his heritage of trust and faith and build upon it. Abram and Sarai had gone decades without being able to reproduce, but after the age of seventy, even the hope of a miracle like the one Terah had received was beginning to wane. They were beyond the age of even expecting a miracle like Terah had. Their land was barren, and the pain and disappointment was deep. It's almost like God was waiting for Sarai's womb to be **good and dead** before the promised Isaac would arrive!

Do you have any promises, unfulfilled, that you have given up on because it's been so long, too many mistakes have been made, or too much water has passed under the bridge? Is that area of your heart "beyond the age of baring"? Perhaps you are on the brink of a visitation. The same God who spoke "Let there be light" into the *"Tohu va vohu"* וְהֹ֫תֹ וְהֹ֫בָו (empty and void, chaos and desolation) in Genesis, at the beginning of the creation story, spoke into the empty and void, chaotic and desolate hearts of Abram and Sarai, and He is speaking into yours as well.

In our story, Abram is faced with God's faith; the kind of faith that resurrects the dead and calls things which are not as though they were [Romans 4:17]. How strange, it must have been for Sarai to call her husband by a new name: Abraham (Father of a multitude). Equally painful and awkward to hear him call her Sarah (mother of a multitude). At times, I bet she struggled with anger and pain as their faith statement was also a reminder that she (yet) had empty arms. All natural hopes of bearing a child gone, Sarah had much to calm in the way of shame. It was commonly believed that childlessness was solely the woman's fault. The name change and commitment to using their new names compelled them to challenge all they once knew and leave all that they once held dear (literally and figuratively). Abram and Sarai's whole paradigm about who they were had to change. *The Mirror Bible* states it so well: *"In Arabic the word raham means drizzling and lasting rain. The innumerable drops of water in a drizzling rain are like the stars mentioned in Genesis 15:5 ("look toward heaven, and number the stars, if you are able to number them... so shall your seed be") now imagine those innumerable stars raining down upon the earth and each one becomes a grain of sand! So shall your seed be!"*

God had to paint a new mental image for Abraham and Sarah. He used their names, the stars, and the sand to help them build a new vision. This vision was not only for one heir, but to build a nation of kings and priests unto God.

I remember at around age seventeen when God called me a "firebrand." I began to look into the meaning of my own name: Myca. When my mom chose my name, she had only been a believer for a few months. She loved how the mineral, mica, sparkled in the rocks and that's where she got the inspiration for my name, or so she thought. Later she found the book in the Bible, Micah, written by the prophet Micah. Micah, roughly means "Who is like God." When I heard the name *Firebrand* I immediately thought, "Of course, our God is a consuming fire" [Hebrews 12:29; Deuteronomy 4:24]. Although we were made like God, in His image, and after His likeness, our human journey is one in which we must unlearn a false identity to reveal our true identity.

The moment God called me *"Firebrand"* I knew that He wanted to reveal in me that piece of **likeness** in my identity. He said that I would be like the firebrand that Samson tied between the tails of the two foxes and I would set the hearts of many on fire. God changed my name from one who is like God to one who sets hearts on fire like God. The dictionary definition of *firebrand* is "one who foments trouble, revolutionary." From a child I have had a propensity to call things into question. I was forever tormenting my mom with the question "why?". Over the years, in my immaturity, I've gotten into plenty trouble because of this questioning and challenging of the status quo.

When God changes or adds to your name, He moves you from self-serving to others-serving. God wants to change or add to your name and so reveal your true identity in Him. God's identity for you is always giving, serving, blessing, and life-infusing. The change doesn't happen all at once, but like Abraham's journey it happens step by step and piece by piece.

Jesus said that only if a grain (or seed) of wheat dies and falls to the ground will it produce life and cease to be alone [John 14:22]. I see a pattern in both biblical accounts and my personal life when it comes to God's work in and through us: we begin in darkness and end in light. Like the seed that falls to the ground disappears under the dirt like a burial, we also go through a process of concealment and revelation. The book of Genesis begins by setting the stage with an earth that had become void and without form. Much like Sarah's womb. *Darkness* covered the face of the deep. The earth was covered *in darkness* and chaos. We have deep waters within us, but they are often covered or shrouded in darkness, and filled with turmoil and chaos, until the Spirit hovers and God says, "Let there be light!"

We find another example in Joseph. Joseph was abhorred by his brothers, *dropped* into a pit, sold into slavery, and thrown into prison. Like a seed buried in the ground, he was removed from sight before God rose him to second in all of Egypt that he might fulfill his purpose in saving the very ones who betrayed him. The woman with the issue of blood had spent all she had on doctors before reaching the hem of His garment. To get there, she had to *descend* to her knees and crawl on the ground where she was *concealed* from the view of others (*in darkness*). Not only did she have to push past the throttling crowd of people, but she also had to push past the cultural and religious expectations that had isolated her from other people for years. She was considered unclean and not allowed to be near others. She could have been stoned just for being there. Peter denied Christ three times before becoming a chief among the apostles and leader of those who would not deny Him. Paul persecuted Christians, was beaten, stoned, and spent years on the backside of the desert before penning his many books, starting churches, raising up elders, and fulfilling his apostolic call.

Abram and Sarai's original vision was like a tiny seed. They wanted an heir (singular son) to carry on their name and to whom they could pass on an inheritance. It was a small, self-serving vision that was not able to nourish more than their own natural desires to have what everyone else wants: **an heir**. The desire to produce a natural family was not something revolutionary. However, when that seed of vision died and fell into the fertile ground of their hearts, it produced a bountiful harvest that was exceedingly, abundantly beyond all they could have imagined.

So it is with our own meager dreams, visions, or ambitions. Often they start out small and even egocentric (benefitting only ourselves), but through the process of our life's journey with God, the small vision dies and brings forth a fruit that we could not have imagined possible. There is nothing wrong with pursuing our dreams. That pursuit is the beginning of the journey toward greater dreams than we could have possibly imagined. God uses those desires of our hearts to grow the greater desire of His heart.

Like so many of us, Abraham struggled with completely letting go of his natural vision and laying hold of the promise. His journey was one in which he had to learn to trust God completely. According Genesis, chapter 17, God visits Abraham again and restates His promise to make of him and Sarah a great nation. Abraham's response is found in verses 17 and 18: "*Abraham laughed*" and spoke words of doubt that at their age they would be able to reproduce. Then in the following verse he pleads with God: "*Oh, that Ishmael might live before thee!*" Although God did promise to bless Ishmael, He reiterated to Abraham that the covenant would be with Isaac and left the conversation before Abraham could argue further.

So Ishmael continued to live in Abraham's house until contention between the earthly vision and the heavenly vision became so great that Sarah insisted Ishmael and Hagar be cast out. For a time we may be able to entertain our smaller vision while God is growing us into His larger plans, but there will always come a time when the flesh and the spirit will have it out. The smaller vision will have to make way for God's plans to unfold unhindered.

Elijah admonished the people *"How long halt ye between two opinions? If the Lord be God, follow Him...If Baal, follow him..."* [1 Kings 18:21]. We will all come to a point of decision, whether to continue as we are or to venture out onto the path God has prepared for us. The beauty of the manifold and everlasting grace of God is that, should we choose to stay as we are, He will give us the opportunity repeatedly to choose to launch out into the deep. We will be stuck in this loop of opportunity until we choose to take the path toward our greater journey.

Take time today to revisit the vision of your heart. Lay it out before the Lord and check to see if you need to open your heart to more than you thought possible or ever considered. Allow the Holy Spirit to show you what you do not know and lead you down the path of righteousness further than you have gone before.

Painting the Picture of Hope

In their names, God painted a picture of the one born from above (Abram) as also being the one who gives life from above (Abraham). The journey of transforming from *fathered from above* to *fathering from above* required a redefining or rather resurrecting of both their identities. Both Abraham and Sarah had begun with a response to the hope set before them: they began to embrace their new names. Long before either was born, God placed in Abram and Sarai the desire to produce life. Then, He used their *emptiness* and inability to produce natural fruit as a fertile ground in which to produce something eternal. Out of their chaos and desolation, came forth not just one or even several children but an entire nation: natural and spiritual. From their natural (some might even say selfish) desire for offspring, God produced both natural and spiritual fruit that has lasted to this day. As with the "empty and void" status of creation in Genesis, God took Abram and Sarai's dead, empty, powerless reproductive systems, and created a whole new spiritual world full of life which culminated physically in Isaac and spiritually in the beautiful model of righteous/just who live by the same kind of faith, even you and me. *"If you belong to Christ, then you are Abraham's seed, and heirs according to the promise."* [Galatians 3:29, NIV].

The story of Abraham and Sarah should give us hope. Here is a personal example: In my birth I was spared from death by the hand of God. As I shared previously, I was in a feet first breech position which is dangerous. To this day, my mom still jokes that I was born ready to hit the ground running. Interestingly, both of my daughters (but not my sons) had similarly dangerous birthing situations. With my first born, I almost hemorrhaged to death, and my daughter Serena was born (after an emergency c-section) non-responsive and required significant resuscitation. My journey from "one who has been spared" to "one who spares/saves lives" has been a road of transformed identity.

God has been at work in my life replacing lies and trauma with his truth, love, and promises. I used to always be the receiver of blessings. Along the way, I developed the belief that in order for me to be blessed someone else had to suffer, or at least not be blessed. Now I am a receiver and a giver of blessings without negative consequences for others. Once I only saw myself as a "stranger, out of place, and not belonging." Now, though I still struggle with feeling like I don't fit in, I am one who welcomes those who are strange, cast out, and do not feel they belong.

God wants to transform your desolation, your unfulfilled longings, your painful places into a garden of pleasure. He wants to make of your dry bones a mighty army. God is not even close to done with these transformations in my life, but I am embracing the journey toward the rediscovery of my identity in Him and my freedom from this false-self I have become.

What the story of Abraham and Sarah offers is not a three step system, but rather a look at the journey of two fellow sojourners. Your story will be your own, as is mine, but we can identify with Abraham and Sarah, and if we will tune our ear to the Spirit, we may find some guidance in our own journeys from desolation to desired end.

We do not have a daily account of the experiences Abraham and Sarah had, but we do have the ones that marked important lessons in their lives. Those experiences that mark us elicit a response and make adjustments to our perspective. They serve to paint a picture of the reality of God in and through us.

As we have learned, Abraham and Sarah's journey began with God introducing them to their new (or perhaps, renewed would be a more accurate term) identities. In verse six of Genesis 12, Abraham passed through the land to the place of Sichem. The word *place* here means home, space, or country and Sichem means "responsibility" or "consent." There God promised to give the land (of Canaan) Abraham's seed. In this phase Abraham is brought to a fork in the road. He can choose to take responsibility for the promise or call of God or he can choose to *consent* or yield to it. At first glance this seems like mere semantics, but there is a difference between consenting and taking responsibility. Abraham's response to God may give us a clue as to which he chose.

Abraham responded by building an altar to God there. From this place of "responsibility or consent," Abraham journeyed to a mountain located east of Bethel (house of God) and west of Hai (which means heap, perhaps of ruins) and pitched his tent. Altars were built in Abraham's time to mark holy places, offer sacrifices, solicit assistance, and worship. From this high mountain position, overlooking the land he had been promised, Abraham built an altar and called on the name of the Lord.

From there Abraham continued south, exploring this land that he had been promised when a famine arose in the land. Because the famine was grievous, Abraham left the land he was promised and went down into Egypt to wait it out. Here is where Abraham finds himself in a position where he will have to choose to trust God or not trust.

> And it came to pass, when he was come near to enter into Egypt, that he said unto Sarai his wife, Behold now, I know that thou art a fair woman to look upon: Therefore it shall come to pass, when the Egyptians shall see thee, that they shall say, This is his wife: and they will kill me, but they will save thee alive. Say, I pray thee, thou art my sister: that it may be well with me for thy sake; and my soul shall live because of thee.
> [Genesis 12:11-13]

From our story we see Abraham was a very practical man. He did not sit around waiting for things to happen. When God presented the promise of giving his seed the land of Canaan, Abraham set out not only to explore the land, but he built altars along the way calling on the name of the Lord and invoking the promise.

Although Abraham accepted God's promise, he must have believed he had a part to play because Abraham is rarely in any one place for long without some kind of action or reciprocation. Interestingly, God never asked for altars, worship, or sacrifice. All these were pagan practices of the day. So, it's no surprise that when Abraham and Sarah approach Egypt, he decides he must make sure that he stays alive long enough for his seed to be able to receive the promise! So, he hatches a plan to make sure he is not killed by Pharaoh because of his wife's beauty.

Everything happens according to what Abram foresaw, but instead of allowing God to move from the beginning, Abram gives Sarai away. Imagine what might have been going through Sarai's mind and heart. Regardless, God uses this opportunity to show Abram *and* Sarai that the promise is to *both* of them. Sarai is affirmed in her importance and value by God.

Note, they are still Abram and Sarai not Abraham and Sarah. Abram and Sarai are starting the process of growing into their names. Instead of rebuking Abram and Sarai, God uses the opportunity to reinforce His protection and provision for both of them by not only plaguing Pharaoh's house in a way that they recognized that they had to return Sarai untouched, but also to a degree that Pharaoh did not try to retaliate. Rather, he sent them off with riches! God used the "misstep" to supply Abraham with all he needed to continue his journey throughout the land of Canaan in a time of famine.

After Abram had made his rounds, he returned to the original place where he had built the altar and pitched his tent. Here he had his next test: *"And there was a strife between the herdsmen of Abram's cattle and the herdsmen of Lot's cattle: and the Canaanite and the Perizzite dwelled then in the land."* [Genesis 13:7]. From the beginning, God told Abram to leave his father's house and he still had Lot with him. This time Abram does not think of his own provision and tells Lot: *"Is not the whole land before thee? Separate thyself, I pray thee, from me: if thou wilt take the left hand, then I will go to the right; or if thou depart to the right hand, then I will go to the left."* [Genesis 13:9].

Abram had learned that God will provide for him whether in famine or in Egypt. With this new perspective, of God's provision, God reconfirms the promise that He has given Abram the land (even the area that Lot chose) and tells him to "Arise, walk through the land…" Abram's first walk through was with his own **responsibility** for claiming the promised land. This second walk through he will journey with the understanding that God *has given* it to him! No need to build altars and call on the Name of the Lord as if to pray for it and claim it. Abram is beginning to learn that his identity is that of **receiver** of the blessing not **fighter** *for* the blessing. As children of God, sons and daughters of Abraham, and heirs according to the promise we also must learn to rest in our identity. There is no need to build a case for our cause, cry out, plead, or perform any other ritual. We have already been given *"all things pertaining to life and godliness."* [2 Peter 1:3].

After Abram's walkabout he pitched his tent, not between *the roar* and *responsibility* (Sichem and Hai), but between Mamre and Hebron (roughly *vigor* and *association*). These two speak of strength from a seated position of relationship. It is from this position that Abram receives news in chapter fourteen that his nephew Lot has been taken captive because of war. Abram, again, does not consult God, but arms his 300 servants and goes forth winning a mighty victory against overwhelming odds. Even with all this faith and confidence in God's provision and protection, Abram (and Sarai) still have not adopted their ultimate identity which was promised from the beginning. Chapter fifteen starts with the Lord visiting Abram again this time in a vision. God introduces Himself to Abram (and God calls him Abram, not Abraham) by saying: *"Fear not, Abram: I am thy shield and thy exceeding great reward."* [Genesis 15:1].

Abrams response to God seems bold: *"And Abram said, Lord GOD, what wilt thou give me, seeing I go childless…"* [Genesis 15:2]. God does not rebuke him, instead, God renews the promise: *"And, behold, the word of the LORD came unto him, saying, This shall not be thine heir; but he that shall come forth out of thine own bowels shall be thine heir."* [Genesis 15:4] After which, God takes Abram out to see the stars and count the sand to paint a clearer picture of what Abram still has to accomplish through the promised child. As we read on the middle of the exchange states: *"Abram believed God and it was accounted to him as righteousness."* Interestingly enough, in verse eight Abram asks: *"Lord GOD, whereby shall I know that I shall inherit it?"* Still, God didn't not rebuke him, but rather entered into Abram's tradition of covenants and used this pagan process to seal the deal. However, to make sure that Abram understood that the responsibility for keeping the covenant was upon God and not Abram, He waited for Abram to fall asleep. God let Abram witness the covenant God made with Himself through a dream. Abram's doubts were calmed while leaving all the responsibility of fulfillment squarely on God's capable shoulders. The vision (or dream) closes out with God reiterating that He is giving Abram's seed the land of Canaan.

When God promises the greater dream, when He replaces your little seed for a forest, He also provides for the care of the forest. God not only promised Abram and Sarai that they would give life to a nation, He also provided a land in which that nation would live. All this, and still Abram and Sarai had not quite come into their new names. Chapter 16 of Genesis begins with the actions of impatience.

Sarai was tired of waiting for the promise of a child to come. Perhaps she blamed herself for somehow stopping the fulfillment of the promise. Like her husband, she was also a woman of action who was looking to help things along and solve a problem. She decided to offer her handmaid, Hagar, to Abram as a surrogate mother to Abram's seed. It was a common practice. Why not, right? She even states in the next verse:

Behold now, the LORD hath restrained me from bearing: I pray thee, go in unto my maid; it may be that I may obtain children by her..." The efforts were successful and Hagar had a son, Ishmael when Abram was eighty-six years old. Years passed before God spoke to Abram again. Thirteen years later, at age ninety-nine, God appeared again to Abram and said "I am the Almighty God; walk before me and be thou perfect. And I will make my covenant between me and thee, and will multiply thee exceedingly.
[Genesis 17:1-2]

Throughout Abram and Sarai's journey there are many mistakes made from our point of view; yet, never does God rebuke them or demand any kind of repentance or sacrifice. In the middle of their stumbling around on the path God accounts to Abram righteousness simply for believing and walking it out. Our journey on the road of destiny will surely be filled with decisions of which we are not proud. God is not moved, surprised, or bothered by our stumbling. He calls us righteous. He turns all things to our good. As the one who embodies love, he covers our multitudes of sin!

I encourage you to pause for a moment, and be honest with yourself and with God. If you've made mistakes, missed opportunities, or done unwise things, I have some steps worth considering and taking;

- **Start** by acknowledging them.
- **Resist** falling prey to shame and condemnation. These are lies of the enemy meant to attack your identity.
- **Forgive** yourself, and if you have hurt others ask for their forgiveness too.
- **Accept** that God is not surprised. His plans for you are not derailed. Your ego will try to tell you that you have ruined God's plans and are beyond redemption.
- **Withstand** these prideful lies! You, your actions, or inaction are not more powerful than the love of God.

There truly is nothing that He cannot work with.

Identity

Identity seems to be a thread that surfaces frequently in biblical accounts of the men and women who are present as our examples from which to learn. Abraham and Sarah's story begins with a name change [See Genesis 17:1-16]. In a western culture a name change, though significant, doesn't carry the same weight as it did in ancient eastern culture, though in recent years names have become more important. In our day, most name changes revolve around either marriage or gender identity. Biblically speaking, a person's name is not just a label by which they are to be addressed, but rather a reflection of the person's essence or identity. This is because the Bible is not written as a history book, but a spiritual writing with the main focus being on conveying spiritual principles not facts.

When God changed Abram and Sarai's names, He was starting a process of changing how Abram and Sarai saw themselves. He changed their names to reflect His will (which was their own desire but taken to a level they could not have imagined). Their new names were more reflective of their true identity than the ones given them by their parents. When God begins to adjust your identity He starts a process that will lead you to manifest His image and likeness (your true identity) in ways you could not have dreamed possible. As children, we gain our self-concept and identity from our nature and our nurture. What we experience externally is mixed with our internal self-concept and results in creating an image of who we think we are and what we believe about ourselves. This occurs spiritually as well and in reality the two (natural and spiritual) are tightly intertwined.

God put in Abram and Sarai's mouths the words that declared that they both had what it takes to produce life, and life abundantly. Not only that, but God didn't just add any letters (Hebrew symbols) to their names. He added **the same letter** (*hey*) to both their names. Both Abram and Sarai received **equal portions** of the grace of God to not only conceive Isaac, but to inherit the land that was needed to house the nation that would come from them. It is very important that we listen to the words God speaks about us and our future, and that we put those words in our mouths. Like Abram and Sarai, we need to stop confessing what we were and what we presently see and begin to declare what God says about us and about our destiny. Proverbs states: *"A man's belly shall be satisfied with the fruit of his mouth; and with the increase of his lips shall he be filled. Death and life are in the power of the tongue: and they that love it shall eat the fruit thereof."* [Proverbs 18:20-21]. Jesus told His disciples *"For verily I say unto you, That whosoever shall say unto this mountain, Be thou removed, and be thou cast into the sea; and shall not doubt in his heart, but shall believe that those things which he saith shall come to pass; he shall have whatsoever he saith."* [Mark 11:23].

Our desires, placed in the hands of God, yield great results as we partner with Him concerning our future.

Even more powerful is that Yahweh, **YHWH** (*yud, hey, vav, hey*), in Hebrew has exactly two *heys* in it. In Hebrew the *hey* (**H**) is the definite article – *the*. Its concrete meaning is: *look* or *breath*. God was placing in the very identity of Abram and Sarai His sight and his life. As in the beginning God breathed into humankind and he became a living soul. God breathed into Abram and Sarai and they *came to life*. Those who are living are able to see, or look, and discern. The mystical or more spiritual meaning of hey is: *expression*, *revelation*, (in the

New Testament, *grace*). God added to them His revelation so that they might be the expression of His grace.

"*Hey*" represents the five levels of the soul, the five fingers of the hand, and is the fifth letter of the Hebrew alphabet. Throughout the Bible, the number five also represents grace. Abram and Sarai experienced **saving grace** which brought them into a new level of living, moving, and having their being. God added equal parts of His: breath (of life), vision for them, and grace to both Abram and Sarai. Essentially adding His identity and creative power to theirs as a reflection of the divine image of His likeness. He put His **super** on their **natural**. The implications of this action being done, pre-cross, is astounding to the religious mind still steeped in sin-consciousness, because in all their failings, Abram and Sarai never offered a sin offering and God never rebuked them or asked for repentance.

Abram became the "Father of many nations" in his heart long before Isaac was conceived. Sarai became the "Mother of a multitude" in hers before she felt the first quickening of life in her womb. The process they underwent was one of transforming their doubts for faith, and embracing their identity as fertile and fruitful. Often when reading this I would focus only on the promised son. I have come to understand God's promise to Abraham and Sarah was not only for a son, but for a nation *and* a land in which to live. It seems that Abraham found it easier to believe that God would give him the land of Canaan than a son, as he didn't question or laugh at the promise of land.

The first mention of Abram recognizing God as the Divine is when God appears to him and gives him the promise. God spoke to Abram and He told him who Abram really was, what his true potential was, revealing his (Abram's) destiny. There are other examples in Scripture that show that our eyes are opened and we awaken to God's presence when He calls us by name (speaks to our true identity).

When Jesus rose Lazarus from the dead he called him by name saying: "Lazarus, come forth!" When Mary met Jesus in the Garden after the resurrection she did not recognize Him until He said her name. Mary recognized Jesus, because it was He who told her who she was! Only Jesus can speak to your true identity! Only your creator and lover of your soul can tell you who you really are! You can only truly begin to recognize God when you learn who you are. In discovering your own identity you also discover God because you are image and likeness.

Growing up as a missionary kid I heard opinions about who I was. I was a fiery and energetic child. Had I lived in the States I may have even been pegged as ADHD or hyperactive. I heard everything from "Get that girl under control!", to "Poor missionary girl suffering for Jesus on the mission field." In reality, the mission field wasn't all bad, but one thing it did mean is that we often suffered from lack. As a child, however, I really did not feel it as a lack. I took my cues from my parents who chose to see every adverse situation as an opportunity for God to provide a miracle. We lived by faith. We were dependent on the free-will offerings (sometimes of strangers) of individuals and churches not only to do the work of the ministry but also to live. When churches and people in the United States did not support us, local believers (sometimes unbelievers) would show up with exactly what we needed when we needed it. I learned that God is faithful and not limited in how He can supply for His children.

When I came to the United States, though I did not realize it at the time, I bought into the poverty mentality. The emphasis on money and material possessions as being the only kind of giving cheapened all that I had given on the mission field. Although I had a job and earned my own money, tithed and gave offerings, and had my needs met I still saw myself as the benefactor of benevolence. I could never give as much money as other people did (or at least I thought they did). I began to not see myself as a blessing but only as one able to received them.

It has been a process of years to change that self-image. My heart could not have felt fuller than that first time I paid for someone else's dinner just because I knew it would be a blessing! It wasn't even the amount of money as much as it was the understanding that I **am** a blessing. Whether the gift is large or small (to my estimation) matters not. What matters is that I am giving from a generous and loving heart. That act of giving, much like when Abram and Sarai started calling each other Abraham and Sarah, marked the beginning of a new day for me. A day in which I saw myself as something other than a bottomless, needy pit. I am blessed to be a blessing and a life-giver not a life-sucker. Not only is the missionary work I do worthy of funding, but my life is also worthy because I was made so by God.

While in Argentina ministering in various churches God showed me something I had never seen before regarding His people and our purpose in this season. I saw the people of God and they were covered wells. The Holy Spirit was moving among the wells and removing the heavy stone covers like Jacob did when he saw Rebekah approaching with her father's sheep. When the covers were removed springs of clear, sparkling water began to flow from some and geyser out of others. Then I saw other wells being uncovered. Some of those wells released dirty water; however, the clear sparkling water from the wells of the people of God came together, formed a river, and washed all the filth in the streets until all the wells were pure and the city was new. The dirty water was only covering what was already there (underneath): beautiful, clear, life-giving water.

Later, I found out that much corruption in the country was being uncovered. All the way up to the former presidents and many high ranking officials. God truly was uncovering the wells, the sources of what was filling the city and He was making active His Bride to bring forth a revival, renewal, and refreshing. In a place of hopelessness, the people of God rise up with a hope that is against all hope. The underlying message of it all, was that even those who were perceived to be corrupt, under it all, had a pure well. All that is needed is for someone to uncover it and speak life.

In the past my religious mind would have missed two very important details in this vision. First, the dirty water did not contaminate the clean water but was purified by it Second, the wells that were spewing dirty water were not destroyed or washed away, but purified and became clean water wells. Our purpose as wells of living water is not to expose, remove, or destroy what is polluted but to purify and redeem it. Like Jesus, we are called to forgiveness and reconciliation and to turn water into wine.

What word has God placed in your heart concerning your destiny? Is there an aspect of how you see yourself (identity) that needs to change? God is uncovering the wells of your soul to bring forth rivers of living water that will refresh, renew, redeem, and restore all that has been burned or corrupted. There is an aspect of God's nature that He has added to your name, which is a well or fountain of living water. This characteristic or trait is part of your identity because you are made in His image and likeness. Like my tendency to challenge the status quo, as a firebrand. Embrace it fully from the vantage point of redemption!

Like Abram and Sarai, begin to walk this new land. Get to know the well that is you. Take the seed of what you are now able to perceive, water it with your words, and act on it in faith. God will develop that seed of desire and passion into a fruitful tree which you never could have imagined to ask or think. As with Abraham and Sarah, God is seeking to restore to the believers their true identity. We are on a journey back to the beginning, the original design. The Garden of Eden and the cool of the day await us again.

Jesus came and died on the cross with the purpose in

mind of seeking and saving *"that which was lost."* [see Luke 19:10]. All that has come before, every trial, every lesson, every victory, and every failure has been toward this end: restored identity. The Holy Spirit is calling out of you, into manifestation, your true nature: made in the image and likeness of your Heavenly Father. Arise, man and woman of God! Lift up your eyes and behold the land before you. He has given it all as your inheritance. Walk the land, live the dream, and grow into your possession. Take your place beside the lover of your soul.

Take some time here and now to ask the Lord what He says about you. Be courageous and listen for He has for you a name, an identity, a quality that needs to be brought to the light. When He speaks, accept, embrace, and repeat it often. Allow God's definition of you to become your definition of you as well.

Everyday Miracles

When Abraham and Sarah set off on their journey to a place God would show them, they likely had no idea how important each step on their journey was. Every day they set out, going about their daily tasks and exploring the land God would give them without realizing that they were creating a future not only for themselves but for generations. This is how it is for most of us on most days. We get up, we go to work (whatever that looks like), we come home, and we do it all over the next day. We do our thing.

Then, occasionally, something will happen. Someone will say something. We'll have a spiritual encounter. The clouds will momentarily part, and what used to be mundane becomes divine. We suddenly recognize the everyday miracle in the moment. Then the moment passes and we carry on. Although a deposit was made, if we do not take the time to purposefully acknowledge and grasp it, we go back to the usual routine and the memory fades leaving us essentially unchanged.

My understanding from reading after researchers is that if we do not hold onto a thought for a minimum of 10 seconds we will forget it. It will not pass into our long term memory. Unfortunately, the average attention span of an American adult is about 8 seconds. Do you know what the average attention span of a goldfish is? Nine-seconds. We have to be intentional about seizing those spiritually lucid moments. When I learned this the phrase "redeeming the time for the days are evil" came into a different focus.

One day, I was sitting in our psychiatrist's office with our son, Ben, for his quarterly appointment. Ben has severe autism and requires medication to keep the OCD, sensory deregulation, and anxiety in check. It was a day like any other. In my usual routine. I did not spend any extra time in prayer or set out with any purpose other than to renew his prescriptions. I did not set out with a spiritual purpose in mind. It was just time for Ben's quarterly psych appointment. Ben started having a melt down during the appointment, also not a rare occurrence. I did our usual de-escalation routine, guiding Ben through deep breaths, then counting to ten, followed by some deep pressure (called brushing) joint compressions. It's really almost automatic because he has meltdowns daily. It didn't last long. Maybe a minute or two, tops. When we were done, he was calm again and I redirected my attention to the psychiatrist's questions. She smiled at me and said: "That was beautiful. Well done."

I have never considered our process beautiful. Necessary, yes, or functional even. On bad days, exhausting, and on good days, efficient. Her statement made me stop and really consider what it is that I do for and with Ben every day. I am his external and internal emotional regulator. Like a pacemaker on a person with a heart condition or an insulin pump on a diabetic. Granted, one of his meltdowns usually would not be life threatening; some could be, left unchecked and unregulated. The point being is that every time my husband, Ben's older siblings, or I help bring peace to his soul, a miracle occurs. It is the calming of an internal storm that to him is uncontrollable. He yells, screams, cries, bites his fingers, or hits himself, and occassionally throws things. To help him come to peace, I have to control my own emotions. I have to calm my own storm. I have to stop caring about how his actions damage things that he throws and how they make me look (as his parent). I have to lay down my pride, ego, and desires for the moment so that his needs can be met.

When we help another human being deal with circumstances they cannot handle on their own, no matter how big or small, we create beauty. We reflect the image and likeness of the Holy Spirit. We become Jesus' hands, feet, and heart; in the flesh, on this earth. *"Greater love has no man than this, that a man lay down his life for his friend."* [John 15:13]. When we lay down our own wants, needs, and desires, **miracles happen**.

During prayer shortly after this incident, the Holy Spirit told me "There are no large or small miracles. What we perceive as size, results from the value or meaning we place on the miracle and the scope of the effects of the miracle."

The example God gave me was pregnancy. Most people speak of the miracle of birth, and those who have the privilege of watching a child be born describe it as a miracle. Interestingly, fewer people consider conception as miraculous. The actual birth of the child is the result of many miraculous processes each of which, if interrupted would change the final resulting miracle. The very fact that a child is conceived is a defeating of the odds. Each time the cells split and multiply and develop all the parts that form a functional body a miracle is occurring. All these small miracles are only perceived as small (or less miraculous) because they remain mostly concealed, hidden within the mother's womb. However, without these small **process miracles** there cannot be the more visible birth miracle. So it is with all miracles. The majority of the miracle happens in concealment.

Don't take those little or routine things for granted. Stop and appreciate the beauty you are creating by just being you! Like Abraham and Sarah, we are all on a miraculous journey toward a city whose builder and maker is God. Similar to the building of a child's body in the womb, our destiny is developing as by the Hand of God. Even those every day, routine, have-to-do-it-to-live things become part of God's creative process in and through you when you acknowledge and recognize them as steps on the path of righteousness. So, the next time someone comments on your routine-ness calling it *beautiful*, *awesome*, *amazing*, or even "I could never," recognize it for what it truly is: an opportunity to see the everyday miracle of the journey that is you.

As God restores our identity, opening our eyes to the reality of our purpose, we begin to recognize all the miracles He is performing in and through us. When we have eyes to see the miraculous, the miraculous is all around us. We can begin to cooperate with the plan of God and stop laughing when He declares that we will do those impossible, big birth miracles in our lives and in the lives of others. For Abram and Sarai, every time God granted them victory against other armies, delivered Sarai unharmed out of the hands of a king, and prospered them beyond what was normal, He was building in them the image and vision of faith needed to bring forth the promised son. When we walk in our identity, just doing our thing, God's light and life shines through even when we are not intentionally focusing on it.

One example of this happened when I was living in Traverse City, Michigan. My parents were coming off the field so that they could begin to travel to more nations and God directed them to establish a new base in the United States. It was my job to find them a place to rent so they could focus on the transition. I contacted a realtor and he picked me up to show me a few options. As we talked about what we were looking for I shared that my parents were missionaries and a little about growing up outside the United States. The conversation was very brief and after two or three outings we found a place and I did not see him again.

A few years later, my husband and I were assisting another church as Associate Ministers, Worship Leaders, and Youth Organizers. We were there to help transition the church as it had gone through a split and lost some leadership. One Sunday morning, while leading worship, a man walked in the service. I vaguely recognized him, but continued on with the worship. Later he asked if he could share a testimony and the pastor allowed it. Turns out the man was the realtor I had used to find my parents' apartment. He testified the few days we spent together, he saw the light of God in me and decided to give his life back to the Lord.

Another time, while on a missions trip in Argentina I was shaking hands and greeting people before the service. I walked up to an elderly woman who remained in her seat. I could tell she wanted to greet me but was having trouble standing so I went to her and greeted her. She shared that her knee was hurting and she had an appointment with the doctor later in the week to get a knee brace. We talked a bit longer and she said she was believing for healing. I responded "Be it unto you according to your faith!" This was a common expression (in Spanish) at this church.

Later in the week, I was speaking at a women's meeting and up she walks acting "footloose and fancy free". I thought she must have gotten the brace, but no! She reported that God had healed her sometime during the service! She wasn't sure when it happened because she was focused on the message I was preaching, but when we opened up the altars for prayer at the end of the service she got up and had no trouble walking. She had to leave to deal with a family emergency and was so glad to see me at the women's meeting so she could tell me what God had done.

Take some time to reflect on all that God has brought you through. Every circumstance and victory you have overcome is a breeding ground for Him to produce miracles not only for you but those around you. Every miracle, small and large, significant to many or only to you is a stone in your spiritual foundation leading up to the purpose of God, and your eventual realization of your identity in Him. Embrace and appreciate each one. Allow them to paint the picture of who God says you are. Pray for God to give you eyes that see the spiritual reality in and around you. Ask for ears that are sensitive to hear His leading. Declare that you have a heart that is open, willing, and understanding of God, yourself, and others.

Against All Hope

In addressing the Romans, Paul, speaking of Abraham says: "Against all hope, Abraham in hope believed and so became the father of many nations, just as it had been said to him, So shall your offspring be." [Romans 4:18, NIV] Both Abraham and Sarah had to see themselves as producers of life before they could manifest the promise of God in the natural. One way to build an "inner picture" or vision is through speaking. When we talk (internally or externally) about something often, developing the topic, we begin to paint a picture of it. The more we devote ourselves to it, the more the vision deepens imbedding itself into our conscious and subconscious minds.

When our view of God, ourselves, and the world around us expands beyond our religious and cultural boundaries what once seemed impossible becomes inevitable. When we finally see with those spiritual eyes, what once seemed inconceivably impossible becomes the unavoidable, inevitable, and undeniable outcome.

Years of barrenness had left Abraham and Sarah with a deeply ingrained and well developed picture of themselves that was contrary to the promises of God. Imagine month after month for decades the answer to the longing of their hearts was a resounding *no*. *"Hope deferred makes the heart sick, but a longing fulfilled is a tree of life."* [Proverbs 13:12, NIV]. A sick heart cannot perceive an identity of fruitfulness and blessing. A sick heart is hopeless. Hopelessness is in many ways a deeply embedded case of forgotten identity.

When we forget who we are, what we were created for, and who it is that does the work then we begin to try to make ourselves happy and fulfilled through our own endeavors. We get wrapped up and consumed with outward works, religious rituals, and egoistic self-gratification. Like Sarai, we convince ourselves (and others) that Hagar is the logical choice. We win people over to our case and derail them from their own journeys of destiny as well. Instead of being life-givers ourselves, we look for someone else to use or do it for us.

Should we resort to using other people who are not included in God's plans we create contention for ourselves and for them. Using others for our own purposes, even godly ones, is part of our false identity. I became keenly aware of this dysfunctional behavior when our son Benjamin was little. Our son Ben was diagnosed with autism at age three. He was almost completely nonverbal for the first ten years of his life. Unlike our other children, who (even pre-speaking) would get an adult's attention (often through eye contact) and point to what they wanted, when Ben wanted something he would grab the nearest adult by the arm and make their hand point to the object of his desire. He used other people more as tools than as people to be interacted with. His neurological disorder kept him from truly connecting with others, something he continues to struggle with to this day.

Relationship and connection is the pathway to reaching our goals. Whether that is relationship and connection with God only or with God and others (most often the case), we are meant to grow, learn, and reach our goals within the community. The process God has us in We must "unravel" from our own self-help, earn-it systems and reconnect with our God-identity and oneness in Christ. The prophet Isaiah said: *"They that wait upon the LORD shall renew their strength."* [Isaiah 40:31]. The word wait (*kavah*) means to *twist* or *weave*. Think of strands of a rope making a tool capable of holding a heavy load securely. The word for hope (*tikvah*) comes from the word for wait (*kavah*). When we wait on the Lord, becoming entwined and woven together, we are strengthened for carrying the load and the product is hope. To help Abram and Sarai along, God changed their names and put in their mouths a way to speak often of God's reality for them. This is where **confession** comes in. Not as a matter of works, but as a matter of building (or rebuilding) that inner picture of God's reality for you. They needed to be unraveled with their false identity and joined with their heavenly, image and likeness, God-identity.

From a child I have had a call to ministry, missions in particular. When God called me at age eighteen to move to the United States and go to college I felt like a stranger in a strange land, and not in a good way! I yearned to be on the mission field back where I belonged. Before children I would satisfy my longings by taking yearly missions trips to work in my parents' ministry in Costa Rica. I would meet a team or group on the U.S. side and take them into Costa Rica. There I would work as an interpreter and sometimes as a guest speaker. I lived for those 10 days, and then I would return to my "prison" in the United States. When I started having children, those trips ended for about seven years. I thought I was going to die!

One day, I was praying. Really I was complaining to God, bemoaning my circumstances and limitations. The Holy Spirit told me to "Get up! Put your babies in the car and take a drive." With nothing to lose, and in my hopeless state, I did just that. God directed me and I noticed I was driving toward the church we attended. "Seriously, God? This place is the furthest from a mission field." I drove past the church and was about to round the block to go back home when I saw a small side street and heard the Holy Spirit say, "Turn in here." Hidden behind our church building was a whole community of Hispanic migrant workers, living in trailers. Clear as day the Holy Spirit said, "You cannot escape your calling. I will bring the nations to you!" As I was still learning, I know I did not use this opportunity to the fullest, but the lesson was learned and the message implanted. That summer another family joined me and we had a Saturday outreach in Spanish specifically geared for that community. I know those seeds are still alive and well, and God has other laborers watering them there to this day.

Abram and Sarai learned with Ishmael that some (apparent) success can be found through the sweat of the brow. However, there is no joy in it, and it requires a great deal of toiling and trouble. Sound like the curse laid out in Genesis? Don't buy into the serpent's false religion. This was evident when Sarah gave Abraham Hagar which resulted in Ishmael. Sarah's suggestion of using Hagar to surrogate a child may seem immoral to some today, but it was a common practice and totally acceptable in those days. It's still a practice today, we've just figured out through science how to do it without having sex. Interestingly, God never condemns or rebukes Abraham and Sarah for adultery or calls them faithless. He simply declares that Ishmael is not the son of promise. Interestingly, after Ishmael (born when Abram was eighty-six), God doesn't speak to Abraham again for 13 years. [see Genesis 16:16-17:1]. That's a long period of silence. Still, like I learned so many years ago, we cannot escape our calling. It is wrapped up in our identities. Just as you cannot escape yourself, you cannot escape your spiritual identity and purpose. You can deny it, ignore it, and fight against it, but at the end of the day you are who you have been created to be: image and likeness.

At the beginning of Genesis, an important aspect of what was going on in Sarai's heart was revealed: *"And Sarai said unto Abram, Behold now, the LORD hath restrained me from bearing: I pray thee, go in unto my maid; it may be that I may obtain children by her. And Abram hearkened to the voice of Sarai."* [Genesis 16:2]. Sarai still adhered to the belief that God was not only the giver of promise but was also withholding the promise. Her culture and religious background was contrary to God's divine nature. After all, God closed the wombs of all the women in Abimelech's house until Sarai was returned to Abram [see Genesis 20:14-18]. So, when Hagar was able to conceive, she must have been God's choice, since God did not close her womb. Sarai must have felt another deep rejection from God to have her maidservant chosen before her. Their strained relationship reflects this. I can only imagine what it was like for both women for those thirteen years!

Most people have experienced situations when they have given instructions, asked for specific help, or requested something and gotten results that did not meet their specifications. For instance, when fixing some toys at home I asked my then 9 year old son, Isaac, to pass me the flat head screwdriver. He gave me the fillips instead. His intention was to give me what I requested, but his knowledge of the tools was limited. I did not get upset with him, and I did not discard the screw driver because it was the wrong one. I simply put the screw driver to the side and walk over with him to show him what I mean and use that moment to teach my son the difference between the tools. I realize that mistakes are part of the learning process. "Why does it matter?" My son asks. "Can't you make this one work?" The questions don't annoy me. It's legitimate. Questions don't bother God either. Like with Isaac, they are an opportunity to show him how the wrong tool will damage the screw and make it difficult to take apart and fix the toy the next time. God also does not get bent out of shape when we try to follow His directions and use the wrong tools, and then ask Him "Why does it matter?"

This was Sarai's (and Abram's) situation. They were trying to use the naturally acceptable, cultural tools to fulfill a divine promise. Because our culture and tradition is like the air we breathe, unstated, and mostly invisible, we often do not even realize it is there infusing everything with it's flavor. Most of our lives are lived out of this **silent curriculum**, out of the unstated, or obvious rules of society. We call it common sense or common knowledge. What makes it common? These are shared values and beliefs that are supposed to be a given. When we default to our natural means, God simply replies (as with Ishmael): "I have provision for that, but that's not the son of promise. Send it away, I will take care of it. That one's not for you. I have something else for you. Let's keep walking together and find it." He is teaching us that we matter enough to teach us about what is ill-fitting for us is damaging to us and the "other component." He "sends it away" because we need to have a singular picture: God's picture that He is painting in our hearts.

    As you reflect, pray, and meditate at the end of this chapter, take the time to truly, honestly assess your own self-view. What do you believe about yourself that God may be trying to change or adjust? Ask the Holy Spirit to shine a light on your inner picture and speak to any false beliefs or false identity. What do You say about me, Lord? As you walk this journey toward fulfilling your purpose in this life whether it is considered "traditional ministry," your profession, or family allow the Holy Spirit to speak to your "tools" and methods. Perhaps God is wanting to do something supernatural in and through you? Maybe because of culture or tradition you are using a Hagar? Be open to consider a new course of action born of Heavenly wisdom.

Blessed to Be a Blessing

I sincerely doubt that Abraham and Sarah could have imagined that the fulfillment of their dream to have a child could possibly have such far-reaching affects as it continues to have. Abraham and Sarah's faith journey has been the topic of countless sermons. God did promise them that they were "blessed to be a blessing…" and "all nations will be blessed through you…" How amazing it must be for them to look at believers (like you and me) in this modern day taking hope and inspiration from their story!

> So again I ask, does God give you his Spirit and work miracles among you by the works of the law, or by your believing what you heard? So also Abraham believed God, and it was credited to him as righteousness. Understand, then, that those who have faith are children of Abraham. Scripture foresaw that God would justify the Gentiles by faith, and announced the gospel in advance to Abraham: All nations will be blessed through you. So those who rely on faith are blessed along with Abraham, the man of faith.
> [Galatians 3:5-9, *NIV*]

As the write of Galatians calls us to be children of Abraham, our story is also a story of blessed to be a blessing.

There are people watching your life that you do not even know are watching. From time to time I am reminded of this fact. When my husband and I were serving as church leaders a young lady who had been attending the church for over a year came to me after a service and told me she owed my husband and I an apology. When she first started attending the church she noticed how polite and loving my husband and I are to each other and she told her friends that we were faking and putting on airs. She ended up working alongside us in various areas of ministry and saw that what she observed was our norm. She had herself come out of a bad relationship and had never seen such lack of competition in a couple, combined with the support and respect we have for each other. Just observing our lives brought some healing to her heart and hope that she too could have a healthy, loving, and fulfilling relationship.

On another occasion, a man who came forward to share how he came back to Christ after my husband and I had finished leading worship at a church we were visiting to help the pastors out, this woman and many others have reported to me how just watching our lives has inspired them toward their own destiny of victory. While helping out at another church that had suddenly, unexpectedly lost their worship leader, we filled in for a time. God showed us people in the congregation who had gifts and callings in the area of worship leading and sound engineering. We began to invite them to join us, and through our own openness and humility were able to raise up beautiful, talented men and women of God who are to this day serving God and others with their gifts.

Each time we receive reports like these we are surprised. I was unaware when I was being watched, and so it is for most of us. How many people have been affected by your life by simply watching your conduct? How many countless people have come across your path? I guarantee God has used your life: challenges, victories, joys, and sorrows in the same way that He has used mine. I suspect that most of us have no idea what depth we have an impact on each other. It is our constant challenge to both know and recognize our worth, value, and identity both to each other and ourselves.

> **You are the salt of the earth. But if the salt loses its saltiness, how can it be made salty again? It is no longer good for anything, except to be thrown out and trampled underfoot. You are the light of the world. A town built on a hill cannot be hidden. Neither do people light a lamp and put it under a bowl. Instead they put it on its stand, and it gives light to everyone in the house. In the same way, let your light shine before others, that they may see your good deeds and glorify your Father in heaven.**
> [Matthew 5:13-16, *NIV*]

Everywhere Abraham and Sarah went they were a blessing to those who were blessings to them. The principle of the Abrahamic promise was never about dominance or rulership, but about blessing. It is not coincidence, then, that we are called children of Abraham and heirs according to the promise. Never are we called children of Moses, Aaron, or Levi. These were not only givers of the law, which Hebrews calls *the ministry of death*, but also took their inheritance through battle and by force. Ours is not a kingdom of violence, but of love and light.

Sometimes even the thought that I am being observed as I live can make me nervous. What if I mess up? I mean, what if I mess up really badly? Again, the story of Abram and Sarai should give us hope. I'm so glad that God chose to include the two accounts of how Abram gave Sarai away, asking her to tell a half truth out of fear. Each time that Abram messed up God used the opportunity to show Himself strong. Not only did God take care of them, He also ensured that Abram and Sarai did not suffer negative consequences. Each time Abram gave Sarai away (in fear for his own life), Abram walked away wealthier. This goes against all we have been taught in life and in church. God never even rebuked Abraham for his ill treatment of his wife, lack of faith, or potentially spoiling his plans for the child to be clearly the product of the first two Hebrews.

What a display of pre-cross grace! Could it be that God had been pouring out Grace all along, not because Jesus was slain, but because that is who He is? When God declared to Abram and Sarai that they would have a child in their old age they laughed, they doubted, and they tried to get God to bless Ishmael. In spite of their doubts, religious mindsets, and cultural caveats, God still fulfilled His promise to them. He worked in their lives through their journey without scolding, punishment, or negative consequences. He will do the same for you!

God's love and goodwill toward us is downright scandalous! Galatians declares if we are Christ's then we are sons and daughters of Abraham and heirs according to the promise. Why sons of Abraham and not of David, Isaac, or Israel? We are sons of Abraham because our covenant, like his, was made between God and Jesus for us. The fulfillment of the promise (our destiny) is not dependent on our ability to keep the terms of the covenant but on God's ability to complete them. Fulfill them He has! You and I are the recipients of a Divine setup. God has framed us as righteous in His eyes. All that is left is to walk the journey. Every step is a step of purpose.

On this journey nothing is wasted. Failure becomes fertilizer for the seed to grow and develop into a stronger and more fruitful plant. Abram and Sarai embodied this passage: *"And we know that all things work together for good to them that love God, to them who are called according to his purpose."* [Romans 8:28]. As I pondered this truth new meaning is added to these verses: *"What shall we then say to these things? If God be for us, who can be against us? He that spared not his own Son, but delivered him up for us all, how shall he not with him also freely give us all things?"* [Romans 8:31-32].

The deal has been struck and God has already paid the price for not only my salvation but for me to walk in newness of life. I get to live a victorious life in which even my seeming failures are ultimate victories. *"Who shall lay anything to the charge of God's elect? It is God that justifieth."* God already called me justified. Who am I to condemn myself by declaring that I am less than what He says I am? *"Who is he that condemneth? It is Christ that died, yea rather, that is risen again, who is even at the right hand of God, who also maketh intercession for us."* [Romans 8:33-34].

Not only is Jesus the only one who is able to condemn me, He is also the one who is pleading for me. The deck is stacked in my favor because the one with whom all the power rests is blindly, madly, passionately in love with me.

To Him, I can truly do no wrong!

Keeping in mind the beautiful picture of Abram and Sarai, consider the last few familiar verses in this passage of Romans;

Who shall separate us from the love of Christ? shall tribulation, or distress, or persecution, or famine, or nakedness, or peril, or sword? As it is written, For thy sake we are killed all the day long; we are accounted as sheep for the slaughter. Nay, in all these things we are more than conquerors through him that loved us. For I am persuaded, that neither death, nor life, nor angels, nor principalities, nor powers, nor things present, nor things to come, Nor height, nor depth, nor any other creature, shall be able to separate us from the love of God, which is in Christ Jesus our Lord.
[Romans 8:35-39]

Part of these later verses makes a statement that appears negative; "As it is written, For thy sake we are killed all the day long; we are accounted as sheep for the slaughter." It's important to note it is quoting a popular (albeit fatalistic and religious) saying. What follows corrects this false belief of victimhood by beginning with the word *nay*. Following up with what we learned from Abraham and Sarah: "Nay, in all these things we are more than conquerors through him that loved us." Nothing that we could ever do or say, nothing that could ever be done or said to us is powerful enough to quench God's love for us. We can walk, grow, learn, and live without fear of failure, rejection, or repercussion because in His eyes we already are perfect.

This teaching makes many people nervous. We fear people will take advantage of God's love and forgiveness as an occasion to be sinful and act selfishly without worry of consequence. Some do, and some always will. Just because there will be those who chose to respond to God's love in inappropriate ways does not change the fact that His love operates unconditionally. If poorly behaving people can change the message of Love, Grace, and Hope, then God is not as all-powerful and unconditional as He says He is. Unconditional love is not unconditional if it changes based on the conditions.

God's love for us is irrational. The only way that we can begin to connect with and approach grasping it is to realize that reason will only take us so far. We cannot on the one hand say that God's love and goodwill is unconditional and then on the other say that God is in a state of wrath toward the world or a certain people group because of their behavior. Either God loves us for what we do (or don't do) or He loves us unconditionally.

Abram and Sarai's story points toward a God who loves, calls, and equips imperfect "messed up" people regardless of their inconsistencies, doubts, and failures. Galatians and Romans reiterate this picture by calling us heirs according to the Abrahamic promise and declaring the impossibility of anything separating us from the Love of God. When we grasp this truth, truly embracing it with every fiber of our being, we will begin to walk as those blessed to be a blessing. It says in Acts, *"For the promise is unto you, and to your children, and to all that are afar off, even as many as the Lord our God shall call."* [Acts 2:39].

As you reflect today, allow the Holy Spirit to challenge your religious, moral, and social prejudices. Each of us has an inner Pharisee who is pointing the finger of judgement, demanding that restitution be made, rejoicing when bad things happen to bad people, or feeling anger when those who don't meet our standards are blessed, seem to prosper, or go unpunished. All these are based in ego and self-righteousness. They are not part of your true identity, but come from that false identity born of the serpent in the tree.

Identity Crisis

In some ways the Christians in Galatia were suffering from a similar identity crisis as Abraham & Sarah. Their struggle may be a bit closer to the modern believer's experience. When most of us were first born again, or received Jesus, we met a God who loved and accepted us. He forgave us our wrong doings freely and did not require anything other than our acknowledgment and acceptance of His love. This inspired a love and devotion that made us want to "pledge our allegiance" to this loving Creator-God.

Like the honeymoon effect couples experience. Eventually the initial relationship born out of unconditional love and acceptance, our ideas about God (and ourselves), begin to change. The Galatians experienced this transformative Gospel, and the Apostle Paul writes to them about the way they have changed concerning grace and how they viewed a relationship with God.

Although they had received and believed the promise of salvation by grace through faith, somewhere along the journey they had forgotten who they were and found themselves returning to the religious system of works. They started weighing God's love and acceptance of them against their own ability to follow traditions and keep, as it was called, the law. It seems that our egos are forever trying to impose some kind of law-based merit system when it comes to receiving God's gifts. We think that we are just doing what is right, and not letting people just take advantage of God's grace by doing whatever they want.

We convince ourselves love is not enough. Which also means God is not enough. Since God is Love, we cannot believe that people (usually others, surely not us) will not behave if they do not have some rules to follow or expectations to meet. It is also quite convenient because if things don't work out the way we want or expect for ourselves and others, we can chalk it up to some kind of moral failure or perhaps we didn't follow the right steps so God cannot reward us with a blessing. In this line of thinking we reduce God to some kind of slot machine or impartial judge, and we reduce ourselves to being unimportant apart from our ability to please this self-contradicting God. We ignore the issues of our headship with Christ, that we are sons (and daughters) no longer servants, and that we are saved by grace through faith. We forget that our judge is indeed a partial judge. He is head-over-heels in love with us and completely partial to our cause!

Sarah fell into a similar trap when she offered her handmaid, Hagar, to her husband and produced Ishmael. The Galatians fell into the works trap. Earning their way into God's favor because people from the **outside**, who sounded right, convinced them that they needed to do something more than just believe. Sarah fell into the cultural trap; using someone else to fulfill her part (which was to conceive and bare Isaac) of the promise. It was a common cultural practice. Why hadn't she done it sooner? Perhaps she grew impatient. Perhaps she felt guilt because she was unable to give Abraham the child God had promised him. Perhaps she experienced a setback like her time of life for conception had officially passed, and now she was looking for a way to make God's promise come true. Maybe she felt responsible (we women do that). Whatever her reasoning, her natural knowledge of how procreation works limited her ability to see how God could cause the promised son through her and Abraham. She was having an identity crisis. Though she lacked faith in God's ability to use her, evidently she still believed Abraham was capable of producing viable seed.

Isn't that typical? Not only does it speak to the culture of shame and blame in which Sarah lived and which she unquestionably accepted, but it is also common for us to believe more in God's ability to work through another person than ourselves. This is false humility. Don't fall for it! You are not God's weakness! You are His image and likeness. You are His object of affection and a source of life and joy. God can work through you as easily as anyone else.

When you believe that your natural circumstances are greater than your spiritual qualities, you are having an identity crisis. In God's eyes your worth and worthiness is not in question. If you find yourself trying to help God by offering solutions outside of the plan He has set forth, then perhaps you are having an identity crisis. God will use even these seasons to reinstate your identity in Him and remind you of who He created you to be. Nothing is wasted or lost. Nothing is outside God's ability to make good. You not only get to participate in this process, you must! Learn to speak about yourself the things God says, not the ones your culture, environment, or upbringing (natural and spiritual) have taught you. As you speak what God says, a vision in your heart for the true you will grow, and one day you will wake up and you will see yourself as you truly are. One of the big indicators that we have moved out of grace and faith (a.k.a. identity crisis) and into law and works is when we allow our circumstances to convince us that God needs our help.

Even as Abraham believed God, and it was accounted to him for righteousness. Know ye therefore that they which are of faith, the same are the children of Abraham. And the scripture, foreseeing that God would justify the heathen through faith, preached before the gospel unto Abraham, saying, In thee shall all nations be blessed. So then they which be of faith are blessed with faithful Abraham.
[Galatians 3:6-9]

Many times, like Abraham and Sarah, our cultural and environmental truth systems tellsus how things are, what is, and is not possible. What God was promising Abraham and Sarah, was just not possible. How dare they believe that they were somehow so special that the natural laws did not apply to them! Our belief (or truth) systems are unconscious and we only recognize them when the Holy Spirit shines a light on them. Sometimes this happens when our subconscious or cultural belief systems conflict with what God is saying and desiring to do. When events in our lives go contrary to what we believe it should be we experience discomfort. This discomfort, that the psychological profession labels cognitive dissonance, gives us the opportunity to see reality in a brand new light and experience a transformation. In nonprofessional terms, it makes our minds go tilt. Often God will use these situations to unseat false belief systems that are in the way of our walking out His divine purposes and realizing His image and likeness. Until both our subconscious beliefs and our false (conscious) beliefs are dealt with, they will produce a sense of failure, barrenness, and frustration. Consider what is written in James;

But let him ask in faith, nothing wavering. For he that wavereth is like a wave of the sea driven with the wind and tossed. For let not that man think that he shall receive any thing of the Lord. A double minded man is unstable in all his ways.
[James 1:6-8]

When the thoughts of our hearts and minds (subconscious and conscious) are contrary to one another an internal war ensues and we are unproductive. I remember one such moment in my own development. I was on the leadership team in a church and there was a particular member who was really struggling with addiction. This member would go out on Friday (and even Saturday at times), get intoxicated and make other self-destructive choices. Then, come Sunday, the member would come to church, and need prayer for healing, finances, or something.

Every time, God would touch this person, you could tangibly feel the love, and the member would get healed, receive a financial miracle, or other provision that was needed. This happened repeatedly and always in a way that I would notice it. It was like God was shining a big spotlight on it…rubbing it in! I, on the other hand, would have a need and it seemed as if I struggled and often went with my own needs unmet. How is this possible? Surely I am more worthy than this sinning believer! Enter my **inner Pharisee.** I was working in the church and living a moral, self-controlled, lifestyle. When I became aware of these thoughts and feelings, a war began on the inside of me between my ego and God's grace. My feelings of self-righteousness were replaced with feelings of guilt and shame. Equally destructive and equally contrary to the love of God.

God used this (and so many more) opportunities of cognitive dissonance to unseat in me a works and worthiness mentality and awaken me to a greater understanding of the unconditional love of God available to **all**, not just the upstanding citizens. God was showing me that although I spoke of His blessings as being a result of the cross and not based on our own righteousness, I really didn't believe it. I thought I did, but my emotional responses were proving otherwise. In my heart, I expected myself and others to earn God's blessings and provision.

We all have double minded beliefs of which we are not conscious. Whether they are religious or cultural in nature, God uses our circumstances and other people to shine a spotlight on them and help move us toward realizing our true identity: image and likeness. When we begin to see ourselves as God sees us what is in the book of Philippians becomes much easier:

Be careful for nothing; but in every thing by prayer and supplication with thanksgiving let your requests be made known unto God. And the peace of God, which passeth all understanding, shall keep

> your hearts and minds through Christ Jesus. Finally, brethren, whatsoever things are true, whatsoever things are honest, whatsoever things are just, whatsoever things are pure, whatsoever things are lovely, whatsoever things are of good report; if there be any virtue, and if there be any praise, think on these things. Those things, which ye have both learned, and received, and heard, and seen in me, do: and the God of peace shall be with you.
> [Philippians 4:6-9]

The closer we get to recognizing our identity as image and likeness the greater the peace we will experience as well. We experience peace, not because there is an absence of pain, turmoil, or discomfort. The peace we have is in knowing that no matter our temporal circumstances, our position in and with our Heavenly Father is unchanging. There truly is nothing that can separate us from His completely unconditional love!

As you meditate today, approach the throne of Grace with confidence knowing that you are accepted in the beloved. Ask the Holy Spirit to deepen your revelation of your identity in Christ. If there is any area in which you have judged yourself, believed yourself to be unworthy, or otherwise resorted to works to please your Heavenly Father ask Him to replace it with His truth and give you the experience needed to replace those barren places in your heart with fertile, fruitful land.

What is Your Backstory?

How can Bible-studying believers have unbiblical conscious and subconscious belief systems? Remember the story in the previous chapter about the church member who didn't measure up to my standard to deserve God's help? I knew plenty of Bible verses about grace. I quoted them and even taught them in Bible school, but it wasn't until I was faced with my own subconscious judgments that I truly was awakened to grace and unconditional love. The Pharisees and Sadducees of Jesus' day had entire books of the Bible memorized, fasted and prayed regularly, and were contributors to the temple of God. Yet, they were the ones who clamored for Jesus' crucifixion. They were constantly at odds with Jesus. All their knowledge and spiritual discipline did not make them more godly or help them perceive what God was up to.

While studying for my masters in education, I ran across a very interesting study about reading and comprehension that I believe also applies to our ability to interpret divine revelation. The study showed that seventy-five percent of reading is memorization. That is to say, three quarters or more of the words that we read (if read fluently) we already know and have memorized. Even if they are misspelled, or have letters omitted (or even replaced with numbers), our minds fill in the gaps, and along we go. The same study showed that ninety-five percent of comprehension (what we get out of those words we read and the meaning we make of them) is informed by our background knowledge (what we already know about the subject). This is why when you are reading about something that you know nothing about (say nuclear physics), your reading slows down (new words you may not have memorized) and sometimes you can read all the words and not understand the message that is being conveyed. You end up reading and rereading. Often, if you cannot get help, this process ends in frustration and false or erroneous conclusions.

So is the same, when we read the Bible, hear a sermon, or a prophetic word. We filter everything through our *background* knowledge. What we already know or believe about the subject, God, and ourselves. We come to conclusions based on what we already know or think we know.

Everyone falls prey to their own blindspots. David Perkins, a professor and researcher at the Harvard Graduate School of Education, coined the term "my-side bias" referring to a preference for "my" side of an issue [Baron 2000, p. 195]. We are prone to confirmation bias. Confirmation bias is the tendency to search for, interpret, favor, and recall information in a way that confirms or strengthens one's prior personal beliefs or hypotheses. It is a type of cognitive bias. People display this bias when they gather or remember information selectively, or when they interpret it in a biased way. The effect is stronger for desired outcomes, for emotionally charged issues, and for deeply entrenched beliefs. Often we have to live through an experience that goes against our presuppositions and forces us into crisis mode. Some people (depending on personality) may give up, shut down, get angry, try to run away, dissociate, or escape facing the incongruity in some other way. Others spring into action, argue, protest, and stubbornly cling to their beliefs. Falling back on what their biased experiences, culture, and religion has taught them should be the course of action, they fight to the bitter end.

Even when we are aware that a fundamental change needs to occur, it is rare to just embrace the new or different way of thinking immediately. Most of the time, we yo-yo back and forth, wrestling with every nuance and struggling through the practical has an impact on our attitudes and actions. I have my own painful journey in this area.

I was raised by a Charismatic, Word of Faith, evangelist and missionary. I spent most of the formative years of my life in and out of miracle, healing, and evangelistic crusades. None of it was a sham or hyped up for the television crew. I witnessed healings, miracles (verified as legit), and so many lives changed. So, when our third-born son, Ben, was diagnosed with autism (at age 3), I went back to my roots and figured I would pray, fast, cast out the devil, and declare healing. I could see the headlines in the papers: "Michigan Boy Miraculously Healed of Autism"! A revival would break out in our town and thousands would come to Christ. I just had to use my faith, right?

Turns out that wasn't the journey. For me, or for my son. The journey that I thought would lead me down a path of fame and glory, of 'wow-and-pow,' was a much deeper and more impactful one. The journey that our whole family has taken with our Ben has been a journey toward compassion, mercy, empathy and perseverance. It has been a journey leading us away from our ingrained culture of worth based on merit. A culture and religious system designed to manipulate God, ourselves, and others to feed egoistic need for control.

Small, everyday miracles have brought us to where we are today, and we have a long road ahead of us still. To be clear, I've never stopped looking for that final moment or miracle when all the dots are connected and my son is finally able to connect with the world around him in more easily perceived ways; however, I have learned to rest and rejoice in every "small" win because I have realized that there is no such thing as big or small miracles. What makes a miracle big or small is the value we place on it and the eyes with which we perceive it.

I will not cover all of Ben's story in this book. He deserves a book of his own. However, I will share a few things that Ben has taught me. Truths about faith, the Body of Christ, and the process or journey that we are all embarking on as it pertains to our topics here. My first lesson was that sometimes we need extremes to help us see another point of view and redefine what we thought was truth or well defined. We must allow our certainty to be unsettled, only then will we know what is true because only truth will remain. This lesson lead me to an even more startling and scary conclusion: 1 Corinthians, in chapter thirteen, tells us that really only three things remain: faith, hope, and love. So I began to wrestle with a fundamental aspect of my works-based, control-driven spirituality.

When Ben was diagnosed we were told that his case was fairly severe and that he may never talk, be potty trained, or learn to read and write. This was a fact, a word (at least subconsciously) synonymous with truth. I was devastated. How could this happen to me? I am a minister. My family has dedicated their lives to missions, preaching the gospel, and healing the sick. My works-based, control-driven paradigm could not cope with the possibility that this would be the outcome of all my sacrifices. The only way I could reconcile the situation in my mind was to believe that we were being set up for some kind of miracle that would launch our ministry and add to our credibility as legitimate people of faith and power. After all, we (and especially me) did not deserve to suffer!

From age three, Ben has been an escape artist. No seatbelt or church nursery could contain him, and he would often get out of the house in the early hours of the morning. Ben sees the world differently than the rest of us. He would often look off into the air and laugh hysterically. He only needs to be in a place once or twice and he knows not only how to get there, but where everything is. He has a keen sense of balance, and can spin rapidly without getting dizzy.

We have implemented so many different security systems over the years to try to keep up with his ingenuity, curiosity, and lack of awareness of his surroundings as we might perceive them. Every time he would escape, Ben would have no regard for personal safety. He would not look before darting across a street, and he would go out in the dead of winter with no shoes, coat, and sometimes no pants. At times he would even walk down the middle of the street (as if in a car). The fact that he has never sustained injury, caused any traffic accidents, and is still alive and well today is a testament to the protection of God.

Over the years, God has from time to time highlighted one of Ben's oddities and shown me some incredible parallels to both the Body of Christ and us as individuals. How many times do we rush headlong out into things (naturally and spiritually) with no regard for ourselves and others? Perceiving our actions and surroundings only from our own point of view and with no awareness of the conditions around us? Yet, God seems to just weave it all together into our journey and for our good. Not only for us, but also for the other people we are affecting with our thoughtless words and deeds. Like Ben, we are not intending to endanger or inconvenience anyone. We just don't see it.

Every day on this journey, as with Ben, is a miracle! If we have eyes to see what God is making out of our lives, we will appreciate the journey more, and learn to work with Him instead of fighting against it or just wishing the time away.

We will give others grace knowing that we are all flying blind to some extent. Often, our focus and attention is so fossilized that we have trouble seeing any other options before us.

When Ben gets it into his head that he wants to go somewhere he will look for any and every opportunity to slip out a door or window. One day, after we had not been able to go out for over a week, I watched him check every door in the house three times during one hour looking for a way to escape. When we are desperate for escape, relief, or "breakthrough" we can be the same way. We rattle every door, wandering from space to space looking for a way to cheat our way out of the situation. All the while, we cannot even conceive the possibility that we are not stuck but are safe here.

Ironically, as desperate and blind as Ben was in his efforts to get out of the house, I was in finding a way to make him normal, or at least more easy to manage so that I could do what I wanted to do in life and ministry and escape having to deal with life from a different, unfamiliar, and uncomfortable perspective. Most of the time the people we spoke to about Ben gave us little hope that anything would improve. Others tried to encourage us by commending how we were living with hearing: "I don't know how you guys do it," and "You are so strong!" Although good for ego, the adulations had an unintended side effect: this made it hard to be vulnerable, admit weakness, and reach for help.

I was thrilled when Ben's teacher asked me how I felt about potty training. Ben was six at the time and I repeated to her what the doctors and psychologists had told me. "Ridiculous!" she said. "I've never met a kiddo I couldn't train. When do you want to get started?" So, we experienced our first miracle. Six years old, Ben was potty trained. In one summer, he was doing on his own what we were told may never happen. It took a couple years to get night time taken care of, but we had gotten the tools we needed and, most importantly, hope.

Although the infusion of hope was not a bad thing, I was still operating from a position of works. It had been three years since his diagnosis. Three years of praying, confessing, and (as we were taught) battling the devil. By the time the potty training victory occurred I had gotten so weary that I wasn't praying, confessing, and battling every day. I was too busy trying to survive life with a very fast, energetic, and insomniac little boy who had no idea of personal safety, horrific meltdowns, and did not seem to notice any pain if he was hurt. Not to mention I also had two other children needing their mother. I was tired, sleep deprived, emotionally conflicted, and felt alone and isolated.

The potty-training-miracle revived me, and I got back on the works wagon of faith-confession, and demon-battling duty. Why didn't I notice that the breakthrough happened after I'd given up, out of sheer exhaustion? We say, "Jesus paid it all at the cross…and…the battle is the Lord's" but then we pick up our Bibles and launch into our prayers and confessions and exhaust ourselves fighting. My next lesson learned (and still learning), faith is not about what I do, but about Who He is.

How does this relate to Abraham, Sarah, and our identity? When God told Abraham and Sarah that not only would they conceive (together) and bring forth a son, but also (through the changing of their names) that they would be parents to many nations, Abraham and Sarah's background knowledge (like mine) got in the way and twisted the message around. What was the background knowledge that was interfering with God's plan? Abraham & Sarah's natural knowledge of procreation, and the common tradition of using surrogates when a woman was barren to name just two. Why had they not used a surrogate before age 90? My guess is that at age 90 all hope was lost for Sarah. She had a crisis of faith/identity.

Like myself, Abraham and Sarah had years of cultural and religious training running like an operating system in the background shaping their mindsets and influencing their choices. This operating system goes unnoticed until something happens that it can't handle and then the whole thing crashes! Nothing works and everything comes to a screeching halt. When the Bible says it ceased to be with Sarah after the manner of women, her mindset could no longer fathom how she would ever be the carrier of the promised child. Maybe she misinterpreted God's intent? Perhaps she wasn't an important part in the equation. Maybe God just intended to use Abraham and she was more of a replaceable vessel?

Take the time right now to examine your own belief systems about God, yourself, and how things work when accomplishing His purposes in your life. Do not fall into the trap of limiting God by limiting yourself. Consider the possibility that God may want to challenge your presuppositions. Don't be afraid to take a second or even third look at what you believe. Do those beliefs line up with what God is saying to and about you? Do they align with what you are living and experiencing right now? If not, lay them on the altar and allow the Holy Spirit to change, replace, or modify as needed. One of the greatest skills we can develop as followers of Christ is the art of letting go. The second is to acknowledge and then remove the limitations we have placed on God and His ability to work in and through us.

Faith, the Journey

Abraham and Sarah had to walk a journey out of their background knowledge and into the new revelation of a miracle child. This journey, was not a new one for them. Abraham (and by extension Sarah) had walked a similar path when they split from Lot, and again when Abraham gave Sarah away to the king of Egypt for fear that he would kill Abraham so that he could take Sarah anyway.

In the split from Lot, Abraham had to walk out of his relational background knowledge with his nephew. Technically, if Lot had children while in Abraham's house, Abraham could culturally consider them as his sons, and therefore technically have the fulfillment of the promised child. His culture taught him that Sarah was not vital for the family name to be carried on. His seed was the one that mattered. Sarah believed this too. Even as early as Genesis we see God working toward reestablishing the value of His women and their place in redemption's plans. Often we try to fulfill our purpose and work out God's plans within the limits of our cultural and religious norms.

I remember when God began to speak to my husband and I about moving to another city and beginning our journey toward establishing our ministry in missions. The church and religious circle we found ourselves in at the time taught strongly that God would speak to your elders first, and you were to wait until they confirmed what you were supposed to do in ministry before launching out. It was considered *unauthorized*, *rogue*, and *rebellious* to just obey God willy-nilly. In order for you to be doing it the right way you had to be sent out by leadership. God wasn't talking to them about it, and eventually we set out anyway though we did delay quite a while. I remember wondering if we had left sooner would we be further along. Did we miss some vital connection? Fear still plagued me, but I refused to stop moving because of it. Erroneously, I thought that faith was moving ahead with what God wants you to do even though you are afraid. Although noble, that's not faith, that's courage. The story of Abraham teaches us that God is not limited by our bad choices. God keeps us as we journey out of our backgrounds and traditions and into His planned path for us.

With the king, Abraham was learning to trust God as he journeyed looking for the land that God would show him. God promised that He would bless those who blessed Abraham and curse those who cursed Abraham. When Abraham gave Sarah to the king, God was showing that He indeed would protect the covenant. He was also trying to teach Sarah that she was not dispensable. Sarah was a vital component of God's plan. All these experiences (and many more) were bringing Abraham (and Sarah) closer and closer to trusting God with the things (people) that mattered most to him. These were Abraham and Sarah's journeys of faith that allowed them to see the city whose builder and maker is God.

Interestingly, although Abraham did some things that were contrary to the covenant (like giving Sarah away), God never chastised him.

And the scripture was fulfilled that says, "Abraham believed God, and it was credited to him as righteousness," and he was called God's friend.
[James 2:23]

Now faith is confidence in what we hope for and assurance about what we do not see. This is what the ancients were commended for.
[Hebrews 11:1-2 *NIV*]

In Hebrews, Abraham is listed in what we call the Hall of Faith. In the same chapter faith is defined. As you read this chapter of Hebrews you see that rather than point out his errors, God commends both Abraham and Sarah for their faith.

Faith, or faithfulness, and righteousness are connected. Look at the word **righteousness** in Biblical Hebrew (how Abraham and the writers of both the Old and New Testament would have received it). It means :*to walk the path of God."* With this in mind reading James [2:23] might better be understood as: "*Abraham agreed with God and began to walk the path as God's friend.*" It is time that the Body of Christ demystify faith. To begin seeing it as an outworking of our abiding trust in the God who loves us so radically and unconditionally that He moves Heaven and Earth to ensure that we have rivers in the dessert, highways in the wilderness, and provision every step of the way.

If you belong to Christ, then you are Abraham's seed, and heirs according to the promise.
[Galatians 3:29, NIV]

If Abraham is our example of righteousness and faith then we must discard the notion that righteousness is a fragile thing and faith only works when it is unwavering. We must recognize that Abraham did **bad things** and **failed** at trusting God on many occasions, and still he remained righteous. Why? Through his bumbling and stumbling he never stopped walking the path *as God's friend*. I challenge you to go back and reread Abraham's story. Never does God rebuke Abraham for his lack of faith or misdeeds. On the contrary, God used every occasion to both defend Abraham and teach him of His faithfulness.

Like Abraham, when we falter or fall back into our traditions we also do not cease to be righteous. It is all part of the journey of righteousness. We must begin to see our Heavenly father not as the morality police, but as our loving advocate. Not only is His deepest desire to see you succeed, but He also is unlimited in His ability to cause your success. All that is required is for us to awaken to this reality, agree with God on what He says about you! He made you and knows what He is talking about.

Our challenge, like Abraham's is that we need to let go of what we think we know about God, ourselves, and the world. That letting go feels like jumping off a cliff into a dark cavern that seems to have no bottom. The reason is because as humans we find certainty to be of great comfort. Certainty calms our fears and gives us a sense of order and control.

I love this quote from Peter Enn's book, The Sin of Certainty: *"The preoccupation with holding on to correct thinking with a tightly closed fist is not a sign of strong faith. It hinders the life of faith, because we are simply acting on a deep unnamed human fear of losing the sense of familiarity and predictability that our thoughts about God give us. Believing that we are right about God helps give us a sense of order in an otherwise messy world. So when we are confronted with the possibility of being wrong, that kind of faith becomes all about finding ways to hold on with everything we've got to be right. We are not trusting God at that moment. We are trusting ourselves and disguising it as trusting God."*

This is the place I found myself in concerning my son Ben's healing. Because I was so certain that I knew God's plan was to make a public miraculous display of Ben's healing, I lived in a constant daily state of hope-differed or disappointment. Every day that his healing did not manifest (in the way I envisioned it) deepened my pain. When I let go of my hyper-focus on manifesting my son's healing and began to embrace him as a person, where he is at, peace entered my heart and I was able to walk a path of enduring faith not works-based emotionalism.

I learned that the more I focused on autism the deeper autism became entrenched and took over my heart, mind, and home. It took many years to get to this place, and I am still building a different image and reality of who my son is and who I am. These days my confession and prayer speak more to him than commanding some external force off of him, or onto him. My words are targeted to teach my son who he is because of Christ: beloved, whole, and priceless. I chose to help him build a self image that is not limited by a physical manifestation, label, or chemical imbalance; but, one that continues from a more lasting, secure, and eternal place. He is made in the image and likeness of the Creator. He is an agent of life and redemption and a reflection of the extravagant love of the Father, regardless of whether he ever fits into our culture's extents of normal.

What might you be clinging to in the area of "certainty" that God may want to adjust? Take some time to examine the areas of life that you struggle in continually. Those challenges that keep coming up year after year no matter how much you learn and grow. Do you struggle with guilt, shame, or inferiority? Perhaps God has a new, different, or deeper perspective that will course correct your path of righteousness. Remember that there is no guilt or condemnation. Like the father in the story of the Prodigal Son, your Heavenly Father yearns to put His robe on your shoulder, His ring on your finger, and throw you a party to celebrate your return to the House.

From Obedience To Reality

Abram and Sarai needed to go through a spiritual identity awakening. They had to discover (or rediscover) who they were created to be from the beginning. All the years of believing a lie about themselves had produced a reality around them of barrenness. We live in a culture (both naturally and religiously) that is steeped in lack, shame, and scarcity. We are driven and manipulated by the unholy trinity of law, legalism, and a works mentality. Every religious voice shouts: "You are not (strong/qualified/holy/moral/wealthy/smart/experienced) enough!" There are many other choice words they attempt to fill in the blank with. In short, religious voices will say you are lacking.

A big step in this process of identity rediscovery for Abram and Sarai was when God changed their names. There is a reason that this apparently trivial adjustment was included in their transformation. God knew what was needed to move them out of their known comfort zone and into a revelation that would open their eyes to the true state of reality. As He is no respecter of persons, God also knows what is needed to shift your perception back to His truth.

First, there was a cultural affect that was not lost on them. Let's review. In the ancient near east, when a person underwent some life-changing event, it was common to take a new name. In the story of Ruth, for example, we find that Naomi (whose name meant 'My Pleasant One') changed her name to Marah ('Bitter') following her troubles. Although this was not a positive change, she chose the name as it is how she identified her new normal. Be watchful of what you accept as normal. Make sure that you do not embrace or own a normal that is contrary to what God has declared as His purpose for you.

Although my son, Ben, has meltdowns and still can wander off as a result of autism, I do not embrace that as his normal or as him "just being Ben." These manifestations of dysfunction are **not** who he is. Ben is a loving and compassionate young man. His struggles are not who he is, just as mine are not who I am, and your struggles are not who you are. Never let your roadblocks define you.

It was also common for people in that culture to have double names, for example, Matthew Levi and Reuel Jethro. When God called Jacob, Israel, that name change resulted in a double name. Israel was called by both names afterwards. However, there is also a spiritual principle here that applies to us regardless of difference in culture and the passage of time. What we say and how we perceive ourselves may seem a small, trivial matter, but it is far from it.

We live in a world of an abundance of words and visual effects. Sometimes we do not recognize the impact of our words, especially those spoken in haste and frustration. The good news is that we can choose to walk the path and adjust both our speech and perception through prayer, Bible study, and meditation. The effort involved in slowing down and paying attention to our thoughts, feelings, attitudes, and words can be challenging. It becomes necessary to build routines into our days and weeks so that we do not unintentionally let time run away with us.

The eleventh chapter in Hebrews reinforces why our words are so important. The writer of Hebrews tells us that God created the worlds by the words of His mouth. As children, created in His image and likeness, we also form our world with the words of our mouth. Words spoken in truth and trust result in triumph. I remember the first time I spoke aloud my identity as a Life-giver. It rose up out of me and rolled off my tongue like I had said it my entire life: "I am light, and wherever I am there can be no darkness! I don't have light, *I am light!*" Since that time God is continually adding to my name ('shem' in Hebrew): "I am love, and love never fails." I move through all the fruit of the spirit. You name the Galatians fruit, that's the kind of tree I am! This is who you are!

When God changed Abram to Abraham, He was not taking from Abram his origins (born from above), but adding to the one who was born from above the power to birth from above. To make this journey God knew exactly what it would take for Abram to evolve into Abraham.

Now the LORD had said unto Abram, Get thee out of thy country, and from thy kindred, and from thy father's house, unto a land that I will shew thee.
[Genesis 12:1]

To make this transition, Abram had to leave his familiar and comfortable surroundings. To manifest something more, you must leave your place of comfort, familiarity, and security. Then he had to leave his kindred. He had to leave old relationships. What God was building with Abraham could not be built with his current support system. Finally, Abraham had to leave his father's house. To manifest the new life from above, he had to receive a new source and new authority. A new heritage was needed to create a new nation.

Doubtless, these separations and changes were difficult for Abraham and Sarah. God was asking Abraham to leave his very foundations all the way down to his own identity! This could not have been an easy journey. At first he tried to bring his father and his nephew, Lot along for the ride. We all want the best for our families (natural and spiritual); but, when God says, "Leave," bringing them along only delays the inevitable and often ends in trouble. Even so, God did not rebuke him for not following His directions. He allowed life's circumstances to rightly align him to the original plan. As a side note, Abraham didn't move into the next step until after Terah died and Lot was sent off.

God is eternally patient with us. As with Abraham, God continues to encourage us, keep us, and work with us as we go through the often slow and painful process of letting go to receive the new. It's not that the process has to be slow or painful, it's that we make it that way because of our egos, fear, and need for comfort and control. Ironically, we prolong our own suffering as we cling to the illusion of certainty and control instead of embracing the unknowable God.

And I will make of thee a great nation, and I will bless thee, and make thy name great; and thou shalt be a blessing: And I will bless them that bless thee, and curse him that curseth thee: and in thee shall all families of the earth be blessed).
[Genesis 12:2,3]

In the second verse, God lays out His plans for Abraham. Plans to bless and not to harm. Plans for a hope and a future [see Jeremiah 29:11]. God is forever reassuring us that His plans are good. We struggle trusting because to some measure we still perceive God in a pagan deity light. As with Zeus, we think if we displease or disappoint Him some punishment or consequence will befall us. However, if we take Abraham and Sarah's journey into account, we only see God patiently and lovingly covering their mistakes and reasoning with them in their disbelief.

In the third verse, God reassures Abraham that He will defend the vision and the promises by backing Abraham up and blessing those who contribute to the fulfillment of the vision and causing the curses of those who opposed him to fall back on them. God also knows that we are forgetful, so He provided Abraham with many reminders both through life-lessons and through words and visitations. God also made provision for Abraham's faithless acts like giving Sarah to the King and taking Hagar to produce Ishmael. Contrary to what one would expect from a god like Zeus, God restores Abimelech's household once Sarah is returned and God provides for and blesses Ishmael and Hagar as well. God is teaching Abraham, and us, that He is about restoration not punishment.

God is going after your foundations and false-identity. He may not ask you to move away from home, church, and family although that is a possibility. Whatever the change He is speaking to you about, it is about restoring you to your Garden of Eden Identity. Foundational transformation can be scary and painful. Embrace it. Know that you are held in the gentle hands of Grace!

Similar to Abraham, you are on a journey. Know that God in His Grace has also made your provision. He stands at the ready to cover for you when you falter. He will provide for your missteps, and bless all those who contribute to your journey. No curses will have any power over you or affect your journey in any negative way. He is at work in the lives of those who may appear to work against you. God is offering them opportunities to discover their identity in Him and His great love for **all** humanity.

Take a moment to rest in the knowledge that you are secure in His hands. This is faith. Not great miraculous manifestations or signs and wonders. Faith is knowing your path is sure and your destination was establish before the foundations of the earth. Let peace settle deeply into your soul as you embrace the revelation that your God is going before you. He is making every crooked place straight and leveling the high ground. Allow the Holy Spirit to work deep within your soul, healing and eradicating every false perception of God as a Judge to be feared or an abusive Father. You are safe in His embrace, and all your days are planned, numbered, and secure.

Encounter

Encounter can mean so many different things. For some it means a spiritual experience that is emotionally charged or impactful. For others it may be a moment of revelation whether while studying the Word, in prayer, or listening to a teaching or preaching. It may mean all of those things, or none of them, to you.

While studying the life of Abraham something I noted was that the same promise that was stated to him in Genesis chapter twelve is stated again in Genesis chapter seventeen. Abram responded differently the second time. He fell on his face. After the first time Abraham did not fall on his face. He was obedient. Considering this reaction to, it appears he did not have an encounter with God. Other ways to describe this would be **an awakening** or **revelation**. Whatever term we choose it is clear, in Genesis Chapter 17, Abraham's response shows a meaningful or a deeper affect personally than when the promise was first given.

What changed? One of the most obvious factors is time. God has a way of using time and the events of our lives to cultivate the ground of our hearts. The key is, like Abraham, we walk the path and truly desire for God's promise to be fulfilled in and through us. When our hearts are ready there will be an appearance, an encounter, to solidify the vision or picture God has been painting across the events unfolding in our lives. The Word *appeared* means "*to see* or *perceive.*" [*Strong's Concordance,* entry H7200].

The Difference Between the Two Chapters

In Genesis Chapter 12 Abram *heard*. Then, in chapter 17, Abraham *saw* (perceived) the Lord. He had a life changing moment opening his eyes to see God's promise as reality. As a result he received a new name (*Shem* in the Hebrew). He didn't just hear and obey God, he now received it and perceived it as his true, and present, reality. Undoubtedly, another lesson that time taught Abraham, as it does for all of us, is that obtaining perfection is not possible. God offered Abraham a different source of worthiness: "Walk before Me and be perfect."

I struggled with the phrase "be perfect." Abraham would have too, if God had used those words. Let's stop, take a moment, and use some basic Bible Study tools (Strong's Concordance and what we know of Eastern culture), and unpack the language God uses with Abraham. The word *walk* is a *continual verb*. Some translations pick up on this and state it as "Walk continually before me." The word *paneh*, translated *before me*. It literally means *face*. God introduces Himself to Abraham and invites him to walk continually in a face to face relationship! *Paneh* is also used to describe the showbread kept in the Presence of the LORD in the temple. This idea of *face* is a quality of presence and relationship. God was inviting Abraham to journey always in His presence, in intimate fellowship.

What about the phrase "be perfect"? The word used is *tamim*. [*Strong's Concordance,* entry H8549]. It does not mean moral or good, rather it means whole, sincere, and in a state of openness, nothing hidden. God is inviting Abraham to walk continually in His presence with intimacy and openness. Sound like the Garden of Eden?

There is a journey to walk between hearing and perceiving, or obeying and receiving. A truly transformative meeting will forever change the way we see God, ourselves, and others. When Abram set out on the journey toward

Abraham he had a promise from God with no idea of where he was headed or how he would get there. He wandered around for years as a stranger in a strange land discovering day by day who he was and who the God who called him was. Through the journey, or rather because of the journey, Abraham developed the vision and God's purpose.

For he was looking forward to the city with foundations, whose architect and builder is God.
[Hebrews 11:10, *NIV*]

God kicked out all of Abraham's foundations and called him to leave "your homeland, your kindred, your father's house." God changed his name, the representation of his identity. Then He invited Abraham on a journey of intimacy. One to discover his true identity.

This kind of encounter is needed to change our perception enough for us to be able to consider a very different path, opposed to the one rooted in our natural and religious traditions. Everything that happened to Abraham and Sarah up to this point was preparing them for the moment when they would finally realize that God intended to do something in and through them that was bigger than anything they ever dreamed or imagined. All the loss, disappointment, heartache, and battles were simply stones on the path to a larger journey. What was written in the book of Philippians was already at work even before the redemption of the cross:

For it is God which worketh in you both to will and to do of His good pleasure.
[Phillippians 2:13]

When Dave and I were driving the moving van on our way to Grand Rapids, Michigan we passed a sign for a local hospital and cancer treatment center that made us laugh out loud. It was so applicable to our situation. The decision to move to Grand Rapids was difficult, and not supported by most of the people we looked to for leadership and counsel then. It was difficult personally as well because we had built a life in Traverse City. Three of our children were born in Traverse City, Dave's hometown. They were going to a good school, and we had lived there together fourteen years. It was the place where we had met, married, and grown together. That sign read: "The Road to recovery begins in Grand Rapids." We had to laugh. As much as we loved, and had invested in, Traverse City we knew that life there was out of balance, and we had suffered much as well.

Over the next two years we experienced the quiet and stillness that is characteristic of a spiritual winter season. Our marriage grew stronger, God provided miraculously. Old wounds began to heal. So much was incubating within my heart, but none of it could be expressed yet with words. It was a much needed, albeit difficult, winter season for our family. Then the spring before Serena was born, a guest speaker from California came to teach a Bible study class. During this teaching that I had an encounter, and finally began to perceive why God had brought us away from everything we knew to this strange land.

My identity was so wrapped up in my perception of what ministry was I could not perceive what it was meant to be for myself. Many voices around me had opinions based on their own experiences and presuppositions. I could not even consider that still small voice inside me. It was calling me to something different. Grand Rapids has been my back side of the desert experience. A quiet, solitary place where God could cultivate within me an apostolic charge to restore the Body of Christ to her true identity. Before I could even begin, I had to discover (or rediscover) my identity. Like Abraham and Sarah, it started with stripping me of the performance mindset that had crept in through institutional religion.

The next three years, God connected me with like-minded believers across the globe. People hungry for the restoration of what was lost in the Garden of Eden. This "revelation child" has been growing and maturing to the point that now she is ready for her name. Zoe. She is Life. She is Image and Likeness. She is the future and is the Bride of Christ. Zoe is not an individual, a building, place, or nation. She is *you*, she is *me*, and she is *us*. Now I still have much to learn about who I am. I hope that never changes. I have learned to love and embrace this journey of discovery. It's not about arriving at some higher state of perfection. It's about growth, connection, giving and receiving His infinite love.

A New Testament example of the principle of appearing occurred to two disciples who were walking on the road to Emmaus just after the crucifixion.

> They were talking with each other about everything that had happened. As they talked and discussed these things with each other, Jesus himself came up and walked along with them; but they were kept from recognizing him…Beginning with Moses and all the Prophets, he explained to them what was said in all the Scriptures concerning himself.

> As they approached the village to which they were going, Jesus continued on as if he were going farther. But they urged him strongly, "Stay with us, for it is nearly evening; the day is almost over." So he went in to stay with them. When he was at the table with them, he took bread, gave thanks, broke it and began to give it to them. Then their eyes were opened and they recognized him, and he disappeared from their sight. They asked each other, "Were not our hearts burning within us while he talked with us on the road and opened the Scriptures to us?" They got up and returned at once to Jerusalem. There they found the Eleven and those with them, assembled together and saying, "It is true! The Lord has risen and has appeared to Simon."

> **Then the two told what had happened on the way, and how Jesus was recognized by them when he broke the bread.**
> [Luke 24:14-16, 27-35, NIV]

It took time, but eventually the disciples recognized Jesus and understood that the events of his death and burial were part of God's plan all along. All the teaching Jesus did along the road stirred their hearts. In the end, what opened their eyes was not reason and doctrine, but relationship. They recognized Jesus when he broke the bread. It was from the place of *intimacy* that their eyes were opened. The disciples were able to go forward in gladness without His physical presence, because in the breaking of bread they recognized their image and likeness. Their perception had been changed through this encounter with Jesus.

Often, like these two disciples we are troubled when events do not go as planned or when the results of our efforts, prayers, and work are not what was expected. We can fall into a funk and start feeling like a failure. What did we do wrong? Why did God let this happen? Questions abound and it is easy to get caught up in the what if game. It is through the breaking of bread, relationship and intimacy that we are reminded that we are one with Christ and are not alone. From the place of communion with Christ Jesus we can arise with joy and strength to declare the Good News to all.

When I first began this journey toward fulfilling the call of God on my life I envisioned something very different from my present reality. My visions of the future certainly did not include raising a special needs child! However, my life has been affected and my capacity for love, compassion, and understanding of others has been deepened and enriched. I have had the pleasure of meeting people from so many backgrounds. I most likely would not have crossed paths with them otherwise. I would not be the person I am today if it had not been for all the experiences both joyful and painful that I have lived to this point.

If you haven't already, take a moment to not only embrace all that you have lived, but to appreciate the part those experiences and relationships have played in getting you to the place you are today. Your now was created by millions of moments which were divinely orchestrated to bring you to this exact moment. Each moment is a divine appointment with the future you. Today you are one step closer to unveiling even more of God's image and likeness. One more layer of the false identity is being removed, bringing you closer to manifesting your true identity.

Call Me "Shem"

What is in a name? Like our English word name, the Hebrew word for name, Shem, has several meanings besides the most common and literal one. SHEM sometimes means *fame*, as in "Noah had three sons whom he named SHEM/Fame, Ham/Good-looks, and Japheth/Warm-heart." It makes sense that fame would be a part of the meaning for Shem because Biblically, a person's name is not just a label but a definition of their function or reputation.

Similarly, to damage someone's **shem** is to defame them. In Western ideology shem is like your identity personally and your reputation publicly. Spiritually speaking shem is both who you are and what you do. When Jesus finally got through to the Samaritan Woman at the well she ran back to her village and invited them to come meet the man "who told me everything I've ever done." If you go back and read the conversation Jesus told her she had five spouses and the one she was with was not her husband. Then He offered her the opportunity to never be thirsty again, but rather to have a fountain of living water springing up within her that would both satisfy her own thirst and the thirst of others. See? Jesus didn't tell her what she'd done. He didn't recount all her past activities. He told her that her past did not define her. Rather than recount all her numerous failings using them to speak to her identity, He told her *Who she Is*, by opening her eyes to the fountain within her...He gave her a new **shem**.

I remember when I was working in the church office in Traverse City doing bookkeeping. An accountant had come in to help set up the books and train me on how to use the software. He was so impressed with how quickly I picked up on the program, that he suggested I might want to go into accounting. Over the years I received many compliments on my administrative abilities, but the truth was that every day I was stuck in that office doing paperwork I was dying a little more inside. The accountant looked at my present and only saw me for what I was currently doing, not for the gifts, personality, and design that I was created for. In a similar manner, folks in the Samaritan Woman's village only saw her based on her present circumstance and named her as such. When God names us, gives us a new Shem, that name speaks to our true identity and awakens within us living water for ourselves and for others.

Consider Jacob, Isaac's son. Jacob means trickster, supplanter, and deceiver. All his life, Jacob believed he had to manipulate others to receive his blessings. He saw himself as lesser and at a disadvantage. He allowed ambition, fear, and selfishness to drive him. When Jacob met God, he wrestled not because God was against Jacob, but because Jacob was against Jacob. Through his experiences working for Laban, Jacob developed a desire to have a different reputation. By the time Jacob meets with God, he is ready to change his identity to one that is more congruent with the man he had become. The result was that Jacob received a new shem which transformed his perception of himself. With that new name he was able to move forward with humility and confidence.

Jacob received his name from his mother. She chose it because when he was born he was holding onto his brother's leg. In her own woundedness she interpreted this action as Jacob competing for first place with his brother. How ridiculous! In what world would an infant in the process of birth have the intellectual or emotional sophistication to jockey for power and position. No! Rachel's naming of Jacob was simply a projection of her own egocentric nature that was prone to manipulation and deceit. Even when Jacob misrepresented himself to his father for the birthright, it was at the pressure and insistence of his mother.

At times the influential people in our lives try to name us and tell us who we are, but they are not being directed by God. They are simply projecting onto us what is in their hearts. If we take their words to heart, in either innocence or ignorance, we will eventually come to a place as Jacob did that we will have to wrestle to find our true identity. This is what biblical names (shem) is all about: a verbal representation of our essential self.

A more common meaning of shem in the Bible would be *the essential reality of who someone is*. "A proud and haughty person's *name* [shem] is scorner." [Proverbs 21:24]. In Exodus we read, "The Lord, whose **shem** is jealous, is a jealous God." [Exodus 34:14].

God is on a mission to reveal to you your shem. Your identity, purpose, and spiritual reputation. Like the woman at the well and Jacob at the river, you and I have been masquerading as someone other than who we are. Your shem is the source of your spiritual life. For how this was conveyed in the book of Genesis, it is the cool of the day where you walk and talk with your creator. It is the spring from which the living waters of the Spirit flow.

The prophet Isaiah gave Messiah's shem as being: "Wonderful, Counselor, the Mighty God, the Eternal Father, the Ruler of Shalom." [Isaiah 9:5-6]. These are not labels, but attributes and functions of Messiah. Jesus functioned as all these and more: savior, healer, and redeemer. The thing about this journey is that we are all still growing into the full realization both of Who God is and who we are in Him. To help us along the way, God has revealed facets of His shem to us through scripture.

Our God certainly is all the aforementioned qualities: Wonderful, Counselor, the Mighty God, the Eternal Father, the Ruler of Shalom. They are only some of His redemptive titles, but none of them are His Name. ***YHWH*** is used to best describe God because it essentially means Existing. Indeed, God is truly "unknowable" in the total sense, but we can begin to know parts of Him by studying His many names throughout history.

The plural form of shem is **shmot**. The Bible has many shmot for God which are royal titles and revelations of the reality of Who He is, but not names in the way that we know them today in a western twenty-first century culture. Although we need to see (and therefore experience) God as Savior, if we only see Him as Savior then we limit the "Limitless One." By default we also deny who we are as creation in His image and after His likeness.

In Biblical Hebrew, to trust in another's shem means to trust because of Who He is. To bless Someone's shem is to bless Him because of Who He is. God said: "I will bless those who bless you and I will curse those who curse you." God put the "hey" of his name in Abram and Sarai, inserting the "breath of life" back into His creation. This adds a new meaning to the verse "*For whosoever shall call upon the name of the Lord shall be saved.*" [Romans 10:13]. When we "*confess with our mouth the Lord Jesus Christ and believe in our heart that God rose Jesus from the grave .*" [Romans 10:9]. It is more than verbal assent to the plan of salvation, but also breathing in of the *hey* of God. We too become a living soul and receive a *new name*. The name might be new to us, but has always been our name in God's view.

When Abram perceived the Lord, he had an encounter which changed his very name...the essence of who Abram (and Sarai) – their shem was transformed and they *became* Abraham and Sarah – in essence new creations as the scripture says: "*Therefore, if anyone is in Christ, the new creation has come: The old has gone, the new is here!*" [2 Corinthians 5:17,

NIV]. Remember that the letters added to their names are letters from the Name (shem) of God. This is salvation. This is creation all over. God took the clay, breathed His own breath (*hey*), infusing into them His image and likeness. He took the empty desolate void of their lives and created a garden of pleasure (Eden) in which to be fruitful, and multiply, and to replenish the Earth.

Imagine, the Lord of all the universe married parts of His name with theirs to create in Abram and Sarai what was lacking in them to fulfill their purpose. By adding hey, His breath, He restored them to their Edenic identity. This process is the one God wants to complete in you! *"For I am confident of this very thing, that He who began a good work in you will perfect it until the day of Christ Jesus."* [Philippians 1:6, NASB]. From the moment you said yes to Jesus, He breathed His breath into you and you came alive again!

Now, reread Genesis 17:3-8; only this time place yourself in the Presence of the God of the Universe – imagine, if you can, that you too are truly perceiving God, having an encounter in which your very essence is being merged with Him. Every "and God said" and every "I will…" is not a simple promise, but a prophetic proclamation backed by the creative force of the Godhead. Each word, resounding with the same power that created the known universe is God declaring what *is* and what Abraham *will* experience – to God (who lives outside of time) these things already are! To Abraham, these things are now moving from the realm of the spirit and into the natural through a process he gets to be intimately involved in.

Galatians 3:29 refers to this moment and tells us that if we are Christ's then we are Abraham's seed and heirs according to the promise. He is making *our* shem great!

Then Abram fell facedown and God spoke with him: "As for me, here is my covenant with you: You will become the father of many nations. Your

name will no longer be Abram; your name will be Abraham, for I will make you the father of many nations. I will make you extremely fruitful and will make nations and kings come from you. I will confirm my covenant that is between me and you and your future offspring throughout their generations. It is a permanent covenant† to be your God and the God of your offspring after you. And to you and your future offspring I will give the land where you are residing — all the land of Canaan — as a permanent possession, and I will be their God.
[Genesis 17:3-8, NIV]

When Jesus came He brought Abraham's promise to a whole new level by removing forever every hindrance (real or imagined) that could keep us from walking in our redeemed identity. He was constantly elevating the disciples' thinking. *"No longer do I call you servants, for a servant does not know what his master is doing; but I have called you friends, for all things that I heard from My Father I have made known to you."* [John 15:15, NKJV]. Later, Paul makes an astonishing claim, that we are included *in the know* of the deep things of God. *"But as it is written:"Eye has not seen, nor ear heard, Nor have entered into the heart of man The things which God has prepared for those who love Him." But God has revealed them to us through His Spirit. For the Spirit searches all things, yes, the deep things of God."*
[1 Corinthians 2:9-10, *emphasis added*].

God is not hiding mysteries from us waiting for us to become holy enough to deserve His wisdom. Rather, our very identity as image and likeness means we are uniquely suited to seek out, know, and hold the divine wisdom and mysteries of the heavenly places.

Planned All Along

When we see the word *nations* used in God's promise to Abraham (in the Book of Genesis) it refers to people groups. Sometimes this can also refer to governments and organizations of masses of people. On a natural level this does not seem to make sense because Abraham was currently a man without a country or home. How would Abraham father people groups when he couldn't even father one natural child? Even if he had fifty sons he would not be considered a *father* of nations. Especially looking at his stance from a racial, or even cultural, perspective.

Clearly there is a spiritual and not just natural dimension to God's promise to Abraham. Abraham and Sarah's purpose was to bring into view the plan for Messiah through their journey which included both Isaac and the Promised Land. The nation of Israel would be one "nation" Abraham would give life to, but God said nations. Could it be that from the beginning God saw Ishmael (the father of the Islamic peoples) and included him in the "blessing"? What about the Body of Christ (world wide) as it is today?

Such a thought seemed too controversial at first to the Apostles, but soon God made it clear that salvation was not only for the Jews. The fact remains that Jesus came to save the WORLD. He came for the Jew, Greek, Barbarian, Slave, Free, Male and Female. Jesus came to tear down all the divisions we use to separate ourselves from each other and draw comparisons to highlight differences. As we look across the Body of Christ it is easy to see the diversity of believers across the globe. Abraham and Sarah could not have imagined how large the family really is. I wonder what "people groups" we may be excluding from the family based on our own religious and cultural bias?

I believe that God's promise goes beyond natural diversity and includes spiritual diversity as well. If we are to accept (as the Bible declares) that God is multifaceted, then we must also conclude that his "image and likeness" must be multifaceted as well. Even from the beginnings of the early Church, we humans have shown a tendency toward intolerance of anything and anyone who is different. Differences range from height, weight, skin color, language, all the way to doctrine and spiritual beliefs.

If we are to truly accept and embrace our multifaceted God, it becomes necessary for us to accept and embrace each other because of our differences not in spite of them. Unity, or rather reunification, is at the heart of the Eternal Plan of God. God seeks to reunite us with our true identity, reunite us with Him, and reunite us with one another. This process is not necessarily a linear one, but a wholistic one which has us growing together on many levels at once. Jesus gave us the greatest commandment: Love the Lord your God with all your heart, soul, mind (or strength) and your neighbor as yourself. We are on a path back to the Garden of love and pleasure both individually and corporately.

As with most cases, it takes a measure of discomfort and dissatisfaction to inspire most of us to move out of our comfort zones and into something new or unfamiliar. The ego, or flesh, is all about comfort and pleasure. Abraham and Sarah were willing to leave it all behind because of their deep longing that was unfulfilled. David was willing to leave the sheep and face Goliath because of his dissatisfaction with how his people and his God were being dishonored by the Philistines. Esther was pressed to risk it all appearing before the King unannounced because of the great danger that her loved ones faced. Each of these examples came to know God in a new and deeper way because they were forced out of the status-quo. God used their unfulfilled desire, dissatisfaction, and low state to bring their hearts to a place where He could bring new life.

> **Count it all joy, my brothers, when you meet trials of various kinds, for you know that the testing of your faith produces steadfastness. And let steadfastness have its full effect, that you may be perfect and complete, lacking in nothing.**
> [James 1:2-4, *ESV*]

The Apostle knew both from personal experience and from the stories in the Old Testament that God does His best work when our lives are turned upside down. When we are discontent, dissatisfied, distressed, and unfulfilled we are finally able to move beyond our egos and our natural limitations and into His eternal purposes.

Returning to the analogy of Abraham and Sarah, God directed them to leave what they knew. Since their current position (both internally and externally) was not satisfying, they took a chance and launched out into the unknown. Think of the land that they wandered around in from a spiritual point of view, not just naturally. In Genesis, we learn that God formed Adam from the dust of the ground, or land. Jesus refers to land as the heart in the parable of the sower. Abraham and Sarah had to acquaint themselves with the land, the heart, or their internal self. As they explored, they dug wells, grazed cattle, and grew vegetation. There was land that had to be conquered and other areas that were empty. The very geographic area that Abraham and Sarah wandered while looking for a "city whose builder and maker is God" was the land that Joshua and Caleb would conquer.

Think of your own heart. You have areas that are fruitful, fertile, and pleasant. Other areas seem overrun with hurts or desolate and dry. Are there wells (sources of water and refreshment) that you have yet to dig (discover)? God wants to reunite you with your own fertile ground. The ground of your heart. There is not a square inch of it that cannot be cultivated with the proper care and nourishment. He wants you to discover your own redeemed identity in Christ.

As I close out the final thoughts in this book I'm drawn to revisit the prophetic word at the beginning of our journey together in the Preface:

The time has come. Yes, it's already here that the Word of the Lord, the shining of His bride is coming not from the gifts but from the everyday person. It's not that the gifts, the pastors and leaders won't shine, oh they will shine, but they will shine as the bride, the person not the gift.

The Word of the Lord and the Glory of the Bride will again come from those who are ordinary: the fisher, the postman, the store clerk, the housekeeper, and student. The lawyer, the school teacher, the highway patrol officer. Both the overlooked and unexpected will come into the light with direction and revelation that is revolutionary and out of sight. The fresh and the revolutionary is not in a pulpit or on a TV screen. Don't look to the known, the famous, and usual. It is found in the hearts, minds, souls, and hands of the ones on the streets.

Fishers of men, even tax collectors, ordinary folk, like Jesus' disciples of old. You are hearing "Come, follow Me!" Arise and turn the status quo on its ear. You carry the light and revelation of the Lord's year. Not a year as in a number of days, but a year as in a cycle of seasons that repeats (winter, spring, summer, fall). A year as in a growing process with times of rest, new life, growth, and letting go of what is no longer necessary to make room for new life after another season of rest. Not a year or cycle of fear, destruction, and woe. A "year" or cycle of love, light, and unity to grow. For you know the Shepherd and you know His voice.

He leads gently and not with threats. Calling patiently, with a whisper and still small voice. Your Shepherd enters in with the flock, and does not stand above, far away, looking on. Your Shepherd does not grandstand, self promote, or make flashy claims.

What of the miracles? What about signs, wonders and such? Remember an evil and adulterous generation seeks after signs. Signs will happen, they are a byproduct of eternal life. Natural cannot help but respond to Spiritual. Signs and Wonders will not be the hallmark, but lives changed, for ego must surrender to reflect the image and likeness of the eternal one. Like the loaves and the fish, miracles and signs will happen in and through the hands of the many, in the crowd, who are feeding the hungry followers of truthful words of life. No one disciple could take the credit, all they knew is that Jesus blessed it. So shall be this new normal. All any individual will be able to claim is to be a part of something impossible that became possible because Jesus blessed it.

So dear one, whether you are in winter, spring, summer, fall or a combination of them all, you are on a journey toward a city whose builder and maker is God. You have a vital part to play. Just know that fame and fortune and stardom are not the Kingdom way. We must learn to grow beyond allowing those things to determine our value. Our value, your value, and mine comes from a more steady, eternal, and significant source than the fleeting fame of popularity with man. Walk on, fellow sojourner. May you journey well and find along the way that you are and have always been exactly who you were created to be:

The Image and Likeness of God.

Confession of Faith

My Heavenly Father is patient and kind. He is not jealous or boastful or proud or insecure about my love for Him. He is not rude or harsh. He does not demand His own way, is not irritable, and keeps no record of being wronged or my wrong-doings. My Father does not rejoice about injustice but rejoices whenever the truth is unveiled.

My Father never gives up on me, never loses faith in me, is always hopeful about me, and his love is greater than any circumstance or choice I make. Nothing is more powerful than His love for me.

About the Author

An in-demand speaker at Bible schools, churches, and events. Myca has a heart for missions both near and far, and often can be found leading team on short-term trips throughout Central and South America during Summer. Myca also encourages believers via video conferencing in South America on a monthly basis.

Growing up bi-cultural in Costa Rica, Myca uses her teaching gift with students in Spanish Immersion schooling. Her ministry brings the message and love of the Gospel of Christ to both believers and the marketplace. This hybrid talent reveals an insightful perspective as it opens doors for true evangelism. Along with this her down-to-earth, and practical, teaching style is relatable and empowers the every day believer to impact their world for Christ.

Myca, along with her husband Dave, have offered their giftings in leading worship, as associate ministers, and as leaders of youth and children ministries. Often they have come alongside churches in need be it in growth or rebuilding.

Myca and Dave currently reside in the Western Michigan. Together they are building a strong community of believers weekly at The Gathering of Grand Rapids.

Also Available
From Firebrands 616 Ministries

Seeding Truths: Spiritual Wisdom
Packed with Power
by Arlene Yoder

Life Givers
by Myca Belknap

Deadores De Vida (Life Givers in Spanish)

Marriage 21: A Journey Towards Freedom
and Deeper Connections
by Myca & David Belknap

www.ingramcontent.com/pod-product-compliance
Lightning Source LLC
Chambersburg PA
CBHW072011290426
44109CB00018B/2202